Pete Jennings was born in Ilford, Essex, in 1953. He has enjoyed a varied career and is a fully qualified psychotherapist and counsellor. In what he laughingly refers to as his spare time he presents a folk show for BBC Radio Suffolk, runs ghost tours, lectures at conferences and writes articles, reviews and books. He has been the leader of several local folk and rock bands, with three albums to his credit, and has also been a rock DJ, but gave that all up to work for the Pagan Federation, an international umbrella organisation for Pagan spiritual paths in the UK. After three years as the Pagan Federation Media Manager and another three as the President, he is well placed to have gleaned an intimate knowledge of the ideas and personalities that form the many strands of a complex Pagan community. As a devotee of the Northern Tradition of Paganism, he is the High Gothi of the Odinshof organisation, and runs their correspondence course. He is an Honorary Life Member of both organisations.

He now lives in an Essex village with his wife Sue, along with numerous cats, a dog and rabbit. He is, as he says, determined to get his money's worth out of life, and aims to grow old disgracefully.

By the same author

Pathworking (with Pete Sawyer), published by Capall Bann, 1993

The Northern Tradition Information Pack,
published by the Pagan Federation, 1996

Supernatural Ipswich, published by Gruff Books, 1997

The Norse Tradition: a beginner's guide,
published by Hodder Headway, 1998 (republished as
The Northern Tradition by Capall Bann in 2001)

Gippeswic magazine, editor 1992–1995

This book is dedicated to my dear friends Ray and Eric Cowell, as well as all the Pagans who have laughed, cried, celebrated and argued with me. Also those who encouraged, wrote, got drunk, inspired, welcomed, lectured, put me up for the night, got involved, or simply puzzeled me. You are all in here!

PETE JENNINGS

PAGAN PATHS

A Guide to Wicca,
Druidry, Asatru, Shamanism
and other Pagan Practices

Pete Jennings

RIDER

LONDON · SYDNEY · AUCKLAND · JOHANNESBURG

7 9 10 8

First published in 2002 by Rider,
an imprint of Ebury Press, Random House,
20 Vauxhall Bridge Road, London SW1V 2SA

Random House Australia (Pty) Limited
20 Alfred Street, Milsons Point, Sydney,
New South Wales 2061, Australia

Random House New Zealand Limited
18 Poland Road, Glenfield,
Auckland 10, New Zealand

Random House (Pty) Limited
Isle of Houghton, Corner of Boundary Road & Carse O'Gowrie,
Houghton 2198, South Africa

Random House Publishers India Private Limited
301 World Trade Tower, Hotel Intercontinental Grand Complex,
Barakhamba Lane, New Delhi 110 001, India

The Random House Group Limited Reg. No. 954009

Papers used by Rider are natural, recyclable products
made from wood grown in sustainable forests.

Printed and bound by
Mackays of Chatham plc, Chatham, Kent

A CIP catalogue record for this book
is available from the British Library

ISBN 9780712611060

Contents

List of Figures

Introduction

O goat foot god of Arcady!
The modern world hath need of thee!
(Oscar Wilde)

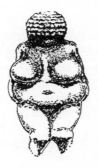

What is Paganism?

It has been said that if you gather three Pagans together, you get five opinions. Pagans have no absolute source of authority for their spiritual beliefs other than their own conscience and intuition, so have to find their own truths by constantly challenging their own ideas, both privately and in the company of others. That can make it very confusing for an enquirer who wants to find out just what Paganism is. Although no one person can have all the answers (even if there was only one exclusive truth, which there isn't), this book sets out to try to assist that process. Inevitably it will be coloured by my own views, but I hope to provide some wider ranges of opinion by quoting from some of the leading figures within the various paths, and examining the various paths one by one. Although they all have their individual nuances, they also have much in common. Suggestions for practical exercises are included at the end of each chapter, as there are some concepts that are easier to understand by experience than by reading about them.

The Variety of Paths

It is important to realise from the outset that Paganism is a collection of spiritual paths. In the same way that Christianity can include Catholic, Anglican, Baptist, Methodist and Mormon, Paganism can include Traditional, Hereditary, Gardnerian, Alexandrian, Seax, Progressive, Eclectic Wicca, Hedgewitches, Druidry, Asatru and Shamanism, as well as Male and Female Mystery groups. This book explores each of these distinct forms, their subsets and developments. All forms share some common principles, but each has its own individual interpretation of those principles. In general, most Pagans get on well with each other, believing that they have more in common than things that divide them. Well-known Witch and author Teresa Moorey says:

> Pagan paths offer ways of rediscovering our mystic heritage and of worshipping without being required to have literal beliefs and lists of rules. Pagans happily acknowledge their unrestrained love of life and its pleasures, but they also undertake responsibility for themselves, humanity and the earth.   (Moorey, 1996)

Inevitably, there are always a few who see attacks on ideas as attacks on the person who holds those ideas. Consequently, as in other religions, there have developed several sub-divisions of groupings. Because of the nature of Paganism, people drawn to it tend to be in general strong individuals, capable of thinking for themselves and expressing their opinions. Furthermore, it attracts people who by nature challenge authority. Such a collection of people is not easily led, and when I took over the Presidency of the Pagan Federation (an umbrella organisation for all types of Pagan throughout Europe) I was advised, 'It's like herding cats!'

Ethics

Because of the wide-ranging nature of Paganism, the Pagan Federation had to come up with some agreed principles that everyone (whatever their individual Pagan beliefs) could agree upon. These Three Principles have been reworded and have had minor alterations made to them over the last 30 years, but have become accepted as a reasonable expression of group feeling by most UK Pagans, as well as those of other countries. I think it is worth quoting them in full:

1. Love for and Kinship with Nature. Reverence for the life force and its ever-renewing cycles of life and death.
2. A Positive Morality, in which the individual is responsible for the discovery and development of their true nature in harmony with the outer world and community. This is often expressed as: 'Do what you will, as long as it harms none.'
3. Recognition of the Divine, which transcends gender, acknowledging both the female and male aspects of Deity.

('What is Paganism?' leaflet, The Pagan Federation, 2000)

As you can see, it is not a prescriptive list of dos and don'ts, but a set of guiding principles, which a large section of the Pagan community use to measure their actions and choices against. You will find an expansion on these principles as they apply to magic in Chapter 13. Being individuals, Pagans may well have additional beliefs, for example in reincarnation or the process of karma, but these are not universally agreed upon by all Pagans. Karma is a popular Eastern-derived belief. It says that balance must be maintained, and that if you harm someone, you should immediately try to right the wrong done, or face having to correct it later in either this or a future life. Thus it assumes an existence of reincarnation as well. It does not speak of punishment, only balancing, although many people misinterpret it as that.

Many other Pagan organisations have very similar sets of agreed principles to those of the Pagan Federation. In the USA, the equivalent major Pagan umbrella grouping, Covenant of the Goddess, has a similar set of ethical rules including exhortations to 'harm none' and to respect others' beliefs and diversity. The common emphasis of these principles is to enable people to live decent, well-balanced and spiritually meaningful lives in tune with the natural world. It is implicit that if a person lives in this way, they are unlikely to do the any of the anti-social acts proscribed in the laws of other major world religions.

Origins

Nobody really knows what early European Paganism was like in any great detail. The few contemporary written accounts were usually penned, via a third party, by biased people with no direct contact with the Pagans they were describing. For example, the Roman writer Tacitus writes about Germanic tribes casting runes and celebrating their rites in open-air groves of trees, but these are just two brief paragraphs, written by someone who probably never travelled to their land himself. Historians, archaeologists and Pagans are gradually trying to build up a picture, but it is a jigsaw with many pieces missing, no straight edges and only a damaged image to go by.

Paganism is a collection of the nature-based chthonic[1] folk religions that originally existed before mass conversion to larger world religions such as Christianity and Islam, which often demonised the older deities and spread negative propaganda about them. (Hence lurid accusations of Devil worship, orgies and baby-eating being forever erroneously associated with heathen practices; the Devil is, of course, a Judaeo-Christian invention.) Conversion of Europe to Christianity was a gradual and incomplete process, not suddenly achieved overnight as suggested in some history books. Often a residual underground subculture of Pagan beliefs, sometimes appearing as folk customs or superstitions, was left, ready to blossom again given the right conditions. We have evidence of this from several Papal Edicts, forbidding such things as dressing up in animal masks and costumes, which was considered a heathen practice.[2] It is pointless to pass laws against things that are not being carried out, so at the time of the Edict these practices must have been extant. What is interesting is that such Edicts (or Papal Bulls) were issued against the same practices periodically, indicating that the earlier ones had been repeatedly disobeyed.

Countries sometimes converted to Christianity, and then lapsed back to Paganism for political expediency, trading deals or simply reflecting the religious values of a new monarch. Some countries had to be 'converted' or 'reconverted' two or three times.[3] Some conversions were just token acts anyway; for example, King Raedwald of the East Anglian Wuffings dynasty supposedly converted to

Christianity at the court of the King of Kent, with whom he wanted an alliance. On returning to his palace at Rendlesham, Suffolk, he set up a Christian altar alongside his three Pagan ones, and when he died in 625 CE was given a spectacular Pagan ship burial with costly grave goods at nearby Sutton Hoo.

The Pagan religions of today are mainly, but not exclusively, revivals (or even continuations) of those earlier religions, with much reinterpretation for a modern world. Because so little was written down, we have to reconstruct what we believed was practised. Because times have changed, we most often operate within a modern context. For example, for those following a Celtic path today, it would be inappropriate to keep slaves and execute prisoners of war, and it might be difficult to speak the language; they could, however, acknowledge the same Gods and Goddesses at the same sacred sites. Unlike the institutionalised Paganism of ancient Rome, modern Paganism is a constantly evolving religious path.

> Modern Paganism is not a doctrinaire movement like that of the Emperor Julian. But it is nevertheless a reforming movement, and it bases its argument for reform on experience rather than on blind faith. (Jones and Pennick, 1995)

The word Pagan derives from a Latin word meaning 'of the countryside'. In other words, the town-dwelling Romans were denigrating their quaint country cousins who were still practising nature worship, while they, the sophisticated ones, had shifted to worshipping the emperor. Similarly, the Anglo-Saxon/Teutonic-derived word Heathen denotes a dweller of the heath, closer to nature than the culture of the town.

Associated with Paganism are the terms Witchcraft and Wicca. Experts have disputed the etymology of the word Wicca for many years. Some say it is connected with the Anglo-Saxon *witta* (wise), hence craft of the wise, while others say its roots are in the expression 'to bend' (as in bending something to one's will, or bending oneself to nature's will). The term Witch means many things to many people. From the nursery tale old hag to the seductive enchantress of some modern films, the Witch fulfils many roles within people's imaginations. The Witch has always been seen as subversive and not fitting in with the prevailing culture, or 'living on the edge' as someone once called it.

Some Pagans believe you are born a Witch, others that you can learn to become one. Some particular paths maintain that you can only become a Witch through being initiated by another. The one common strand is that Witches perform (or attempt to perform) magic, which will be dealt with later on in the book. I believe that this is the defining factor, although inevitably there are some who would disagree, saying that it is more a way of life, while to others (particularly American Feminist Witches) it is more a political statement. They would argue that some Witches do not attempt magic, which leads on to the thorny subject of what magic is. Is practising as a herbalist magical, for instance? Essentially, if you are a Pagan who does not practise magic, then you are not a Witch. However, for a Witch to attempt magic they are likely to have some belief in supernatural forces. Thus, every Witch is a Pagan, but not every Pagan a Witch. (Incidentally we rarely use the term warlock – Witches can be male or female.)

Fear of the Unknown

The moment one mentions the word 'Pagan' (or even more emotively, 'Witch') to some people, certain stereotypes and fears will spring to their minds, if not their lips. Very often the word triggers a deep-felt fear of the unknown, which can produce very powerful emotions. If you are a non-Pagan, or even somebody contemplating Paganism with uncertainty, these thoughts may be going through your head too, so let's deal with them now.

Paganism is not Devil worship or Satanism. The Devil is part of the Christian mythology, and since Pagans do not believe in Christianity, they do not believe in the Devil either. 'Black magic' is a term often used in books by non-Pagans, but has no more relevance to us than Satanism, since we believe it is wrong to harm anyone. Generally we believe that magic is neither black nor white but neutral. Like electricity, it can be used for good or bad purposes, and will be discussed together with its ethics in Chapter 13. Neither is Paganism a cult. The UK government-sponsored cult-watch organisation INFORM confirms this, and specifies that cults generally are led by charismatic individuals who demand absolute belief and discipline from their followers. Yes, we have a few charismatic leaders (I've even been described as one!), but the notion of absolute belief and discipline is a non-starter and would be regarded as a joke by most Pagans.

The other image popularised by tabloid newspapers is that of ritual nudity, which they equate with mass orgies. Only a couple of paths within Paganism sometimes use ritual nudity, and even within those paths it is on the decline. Pagans tend to be sexually liberated since they have no concept of sin, but they are almost surprisingly moral, and the question of indiscriminate sex is not a relevant issue to most. Pagans have a very strong idea of what is right and wrong, but have no theological basis for the concept of sin. Hence murder would be considered wrong, because it harms somebody, but if two unattached consenting adults had a loving sexual relationship outside of marriage, in which no coercion or unwanted pregnancy was involved, it would not.

One phrase much beloved of the more fundamentalist elements of society is that Paganism will 'lead people to the occult'. The root meaning of the word occult is 'secret', particularly a religious secret. Most religions have secrets or mysteries. As an ex-member of the Anglican Church, I can appreciate that the sacrament of bread and wine is a respected sacred mystery, and therefore occult. Are they suggesting that they should ban Communion? I think not. Or is it a case of 'our occult is all right, but not yours'? I am not attacking Christian spirituality. Pagans are not usually against other forms of religion, since we do not set ourselves up as the only arbiter of spiritual taste. We are, however, against individuals within other religions attacking us to bolster up their own spiritual uncertainty, while most others of their ilk are willing to conduct meaningful dialogue. We can respect the rights of others to hold differing religious views without needing to necessarily agree with them.

The British Witchcraft Act was repealed in 1951, mainly because it was thought that Witches no longer existed, so from that time it was no longer illegal to be a Witch in the UK. In fact nowadays the UK Government's Home Office officially recognises Paganism as a religion within the prison service, and pays for a visiting ministry to Pagan inmates. Furthermore, in common with many other countries, it has ratified its support for the International Convention on Human Rights, which asserts the right of people to follow beliefs of their choice, either individually or in the company of others. In the

USA, servicemen and -women can ask for facilities to practise a Pagan religion within their military bases, but their UK counterparts are still expected to attend Christian services. Having said that, I am aware that although the US Constitution gives the right of freedom of religious expression, many States have individual contradictory laws against Pagan activities such as magic and divination.

Hopefully the situation in the UK and elsewhere will change as the recently signed Act is incorporated into everyday activities and local law. Article 18 of the Universal Declaration of Human Rights states:

> Everyone has the right to freedom of thought, conscience and religion; this right includes freedom to change his religion or belief, and freedom, either alone or in community with others and in public or private, to manifest his religion or belief in teaching, practice, worship and observance.

Article 13 of a proposed European Commission Directive on discrimination further strengthens this, and of course the US Constitution also entitles its citizens to freedom of thought and expression. No one in the Western world can forbid you to be a Pagan or a Witch. Nobody within the Pagan community has the right to decide whether you conform to their definition of Paganism either, since few Pagans actually agree on an all-encompassing definition.

Young People

Because we deal with very real adult issues, it is normal practice for Pagan groups not to admit people under the age of 18, or even 21. Originally this was more for Pagans' protection – not to be seen by the sensationalist tabloids to be 'corrupting minors'. The press is less of an issue now, but it is thought by many that young people should be free to grow up without pressure from any religious group, and then make up their minds on such an important lifestyle issue when they are mature enough to do so. The argument against that is that in Europe generally Christianity is taught as part of the school syllabus, and that we should at least be providing accurate information to younger people so that they can make informed choices when they reach 18. In the USA, although Church and State are separate, there is still a lot of well-funded Christian proselytising to young people.

This has been the topic of much heated debate within the Pagan community in recent years, especially as there are now many young people brought up by Pagan parents who do not want them shut out of all contact with their faith until reaching 18. Young people nowadays are taught to be enquiring, and not to accept the status quo unquestioningly. There is a growing pressure, fuelled by television, film, the World Wide Web and even books like this one, from young people demanding access to the Pagan community. I feel that our community still has a long way to go in finding the correct response.

Do What Thou Wilt

Much has been made of the Thelemic Law established by the controversial and influential occultist Aleister Crowley: 'Do what thou wilt shall be the whole of the law. Love is the law, love under will.' Regardless of one's attitude to Crowley (and some people would even argue that he was not a Pagan and did not obey his own rule), most esoteric writers will admit that those two lines have been grossly misrepresented in the past. They are not a licence to do whatever you want. Crowley's writings are often obscure, but what is clear from them is that he thought his 'Great Work' was to do with discovering and actualising the 'true will' of the higher intellect and self. He was therefore saying that one's actions should be ruled by one's highest, most pure thoughts, which in turn should be controlled by love, and it would therefore not be possible to do anything evil. The emphasis here is on knowing one's innermost strongest will, unaffected by external mundane pressures, and making it happen. Psychotherapists can be said to try to attain this same goal for their clients when they put them in touch with what is termed the Ego or Unconscious Self. I know from my own experiences as a psychotherapist what a powerful and life-affirming process this can be. This could also be said to be the theory behind much magical practice. It is noticeable that writers making sensationalist and lurid claims usually omit the second sentence about love being the law entirely!

Help! I Think I'm Turning Pagan

But maybe this is all jumping the gun. Are you still wondering whether you are a Pagan, or how to become one? Well, if you agree with those Three Principles, you probably are one whether you like it or not! If you believe in Gods, Goddesses, not harming anything deliberately and in working with Nature rather than trying to control it, you are probably one of us, even if you do not label yourself as such. A very common experience for new Pagans (often termed 'newbies') is for them to read something like this (or hear someone speak of such things) and feel that they have 'come home'. It often takes a long time for people to realise 'No, I am not mad – there are other people who feel the same as me.' It is often a very emotional experience, and one that I have been privileged to witness many times since my own 'coming home' many years ago.

Very few people are ever 'converted' to Paganism, since most Pagans try hard not to do that. Some people become inadvertently involved with the supernatural when young, and have to suppress their feelings for years due to pressure from adults. Others are drawn to Paganism due to their involvement with animal rights or environmental issues, or through psychic experiences. A few discover Paganism when their original spiritual path rejects them, as in the case of homosexuals and lesbians being rejected by mainstream religious groups.

There will always be a minority of people who are drawn to Paganism because they believe it will make them more powerful, make them appear 'cool' and shock others. However, they are usually disillusioned quite quickly and leave the movement to find fresh thrills elsewhere. Remarkably, in what has often been labelled a secular, materialistic age, Paganism has become one of the fastest growing religions, while other religions such as Anglicanism are seen as irrelevant to many people's lives and have thus declined rapidly, despite their comparatively powerful constitutional and financial position.

Finding One's Path

Of course, there are more stages to go through once you have decided you are basically Pagan. One of those is to decide to which particular Pagan path you are drawn. I hope the subsequent chapters that describe many of the European-derived paths may help you decide, but of course there is nothing wrong with not having any specific path. Some people enjoy dipping into several (sometimes known as Eclectic Pagans), while others feel no need to follow any rigid form or pay particular attention to any specific cultural mythology.

There are many factors that may influence you in your decision over which path to follow. It could be based upon your ethnic origin (is your name of Celtic or Norse origin?) or the history of the part of the country you live in.[4] For example, my name 'Jennings' came here with the Normans, who were a Norse people. Additionally I live in an area of the UK that was part of the Danelaw. I have always been most interested in the Dark Ages period of history, so it is hardly surprising that I have been drawn personally to a Norse tradition. Even without those sorts of factors at play, you may have been inspired by an individual Pagan of a particular path, or made welcome by a group of one specific orientation. There are even fashionable trends within some segments of Pagan society. One year one is bombarded with magazine articles on the delights of Shamanism; the next year Chaos Magic comes to the fore. Do not be persuaded by current trends or the beliefs of Pagan friends, but choose which path feels instinctively right for you.

The Mixing of Ethnic Origins

While being aware of one's cultural roots is important, I do think too much can be attributed to them. We might feel drawn to a particular path because we believe that it is connected with our particular ethnic heritage; however, we should all be aware that the intermarrying of peoples throughout the ages means that our ethnic heritage may not be as straightforward as we might think. While Americans and Australians are generally aware of their mixed ethnic background through early immigration, there is often a false sense of many other nations being derived from one particular tribal grouping.

We are quite used to pigeonholing things as 'Celtic', 'Norse', 'Teutonic', 'Pictish' or 'Gaelic', but have you ever thought how imprecise those terms actually are, and how they are misused? The

British as a group are one of the most mongrel in origins, a fact conveniently forgotten by some racists in their constituent countries. There is fair evidence to point to the Scots Gaels migrating in from Ireland, and intermarrying with the Picts who had been isolated there by the invading Romans. The Irish Gaels themselves were integrated with Norse incomers, who built up major cities such as Dublin. The Celts of Wales, having been forced out of parts of England by the Romans, also took Norsemen as allies against the English and intermarried with them. The English themselves are probably the biggest mixture. Excluding the immigrants of the last century, settlers in England have included the Ancient Britons, Celts, Picts, Romans, Jews, Flemings, Dutch, Saxons, Danes, Norwegians, Swedes, Jutes, Angles, Frisians and Normans, to name but a few.

Many Pagans claim to be part of a Celtic spirituality – some because they know the origins of their family name, more still because of where they live. An even larger number I would classify under the splendid description given by Marion Bowman, as 'Cardiac Celts'; that is, they have no tangible proof of their roots, but feel 'in their hearts' they are Celts.

The words Celt and Celtic must be some of the most misused in our language today.[5] The term 'Celtic knotwork' is applied to any interlocking design, despite the fact that the Anglo-Saxons and Scandinavians used the same artistic motif. I have even heard a broad range of music (including an English morris tune!) described as Celtic merely because it was played on acoustic instruments. Anything slightly fey or otherworldly seems destined to have the epithet attached to it. (Funnily enough blood sacrifice, headhunting, keeping slaves and slaughtering prisoners of war, all things practised by some of the tribes we term Celts, are rarely described as Celtic!)

The odd thing is that it is doubtful whether any of the people we nowadays describe as Celts actually called themselves that. If asked, they were far more likely to name themselves as a particular tribal group. The names of some of these, such as the Iceni, Catuvellauni and Trinovantes, have come down to us through the Roman histories. When you look at those tribes' histories, you will find that most originated as splinter groups from a larger nation located around the River Danube. Furthermore, the other side of the river appears to have been the original homeland of the Teutonic tribes that spread to give us the Nordic races of Scandinavia, Iceland,

Greenland, the Orkneys and even a small colony in Newfoundland, as well as Germania and the Rus of Russia and the Normans of Normandy. So at one time the progenitors of what are now two very separate racial groupings lived as neighbours, probably speaking a similar language and trading, fighting and intermarrying with one another. Then a Roman writer declared that everyone on one side of the river was a Celt, and the others Teutonic. At some stage, one group migrated one way, and the others another. So these two seemingly disparate nations have a fairly common source, which means that saying one is pure Celt or Norse is as logical as saying a dog is a pure-bred mongrel. No wonder some modern academic historians have cast doubt on whether the Celts ever existed at all.

In Pagan terms, this means that although the tribes developed their own particular languages, mythology and religions, they originated from similar sources. The danger then is to equate the Gods of one group with those of another, which is not appropriate. Each tribe developed and recognised intrinsic qualities within the particular deities they revered, and while two war Gods, for example, might seem similar, it is usually a mistake to associate them too closely. Even when one knows a fairly direct lineage, it is unwise to mix up two deities. For example, the Norse Odin and Saxon Woden may be separated by not much more than a linguistic pronunciation shift, but their respective followers gave them slightly differing attributes. The Romans often 'married' their own Gods and Goddesses to local ones in a sort of religious hedging of bets (not wanting to upset the local land guardians) but most modern Pagans believe it more correct to acknowledge the various pantheons separately. Pagans who adopt more than one pantheon or tradition are generally known as Eclectics, and you can read more about them in a later chapter.

How the Deities are Viewed

Pagans view their Gods and Goddesses in many different ways. Some believe in a large pantheon of deities, while others acknowledge just one God and Goddess.[6] These Pagans may additionally believe that all other deities are just different aspects of this original pairing.[7] Others may say that there is one ultimate, divine supernatural force, which is beyond the limits of human concepts of gender, space or time, and that any Gods and Goddesses are merely small aspects of that force personified in a form easier for us to comprehend. Some consider their Gods a reality; others think more in terms of them being the archetypal thought forms of a particular culture. This, of course, does not make them any less real.

If you believe a spark of the Divine is present within yourself, it would seem reasonable to expect that you have both God and Goddess within you, regardless of your own gender. (This is very similar to the idea of anima and animus within psychology, where each gender has a part of the opposite locked inside their psyche.) It also follows that you should acknowledge a spark of divinity within everyone else that you meet, whoever they are, and to show them the proper respect that you would give in meeting a God or Goddess face to face.

Belief and faith are difficult concepts for some people to understand, but most of us hold some beliefs whether we know it or not. The wind is a good example of this process. We mostly buy into a group belief that the force pushing leaves along the ground is the wind, despite not being able to see it. We put faith in the 'experts' who tell us that it is all to do with changes in barometric pressure, and forecast a gale for tomorrow. (So belief relates to something we think already exists, and faith enables us to project that a thing will happen in the future, based on our existing beliefs.) At the end of the day, though, wind is simply a group belief that we rationalise, and if some other 'expert' could convince enough of us tomorrow that it was a giant invisible balloon being let down, then our 'faith' and 'belief' would vanish. While enough of us believe in the wind, it exists. So it is with the Gods.

Becoming a Pagan

If you have decided that basically you have Pagan beliefs, what next? How do you actually become one? Well, you do not become a Pagan by reading books, talking to other Pagans on the Internet, attending moots,[8] conferences or rituals. They may all help you in your quest, but the acid test is if you live as a Pagan. Do you really care for the environment in practical ways, such as recycling your rubbish and refusing to buy products that are bad for it? Do you treat all people equally, regardless of gender, race, sexuality and religion? Do you actually have regular contact with nature, splashing through muddy puddles with the wind on your face in a wood or walking by the water? Do you support pressure groups working to save wildlife, prisoners of conscience and the environment? These are the sorts of action (the God and Goddess directly affecting your attitude to life) that define you as a Pagan far more than your reading list, social calendar or the costly courses on which you may enrol. Incidentally, because we believe in living in the 'real world' (at least some of the time!), and interacting with our general communities, it is better to be involved in general campaigning organisations such as Greenpeace, Amnesty International, etc., rather than starting up 'Pagans only' organisations for what should be universal concerns. In this way we can work collectively and more powerfully with others who share our ideals without necessarily sharing the same motivations. No religion has a monopoly on 'doing good'. Most religions share a common feature of 'being nice to one another', whatever the reasons each may give. It is the end result of changing the world for the better that is most important.

Individual Paths

You can follow a perfectly valid Pagan path without ever reading a book, performing a ritual or attending a lecture. You might even find an alternative way of celebrating it and getting in touch with your deities or whatever great natural force you acknowledge. I know a very genuine Pagan who never meets with others, reads or does rituals. Instead he goes fell running. He reckons that having exhausted himself running round mountains, woods and through rivers, he reaches a heightened awareness of nature and is at his closest relationship with it when he leans panting against a tree. I also once met another chap who worked hard for his local Pagan community, addressing and stuffing 200 envelopes with the local magazine every three months. He rebuffed my praise for him, and explained that he felt daft in rituals, wasn't very knowledgeable and preferred a solitary path, but felt that he 'served the Goddess' by regularly undertaking this task. He had found his own individual way of being a Pagan, and good luck to him.

If you do believe in your heart that Paganism is the path for you, take some quiet personal time to reflect upon it. Do not be tempted to rush and 'out' yourself to all and sundry, or buy up a shop full of books and ritual equipment. You have the rest of your life to explore this path, and you will never know all there is to learn about it. Although it is the natural reaction of the 'newbie' to want to have all the right gear, it is generally better to make your own or discover useable, recyclable items from junk shops and car boot sales.

In fact, you might well find that with experience you discard or no longer need ritual tools. Although the media (and those influenced by it) focus on magical activities such as spells and rituals, they are only a minor part of our belief system. Their prominence is due to their glamour rather than to any importance attributed to them by established Pagans, although it has to be admitted that magic is something that excites the interest of many newcomers. Many Pagans do not practise magic at all, or avoid it until they have developed their beliefs further. It is not a requirement, and some are not interested in it, or believe it is too hard to make magic in an entirely ethical way. (This is discussed in Chapter 13.) Some even believe magic is intrinsically wrong, and should never be used, while most of us who do practise it believe magic should only be used as a last resource rather than a first reaction.

It is likely that many of our Pagan ancestors went to specialists such as local Shamans, Witches, Cunning Men or the priest and priestess when they wanted magic done on their behalf. That option is still available today. Most religions have some sort of magical belief connected with them, even if they are called by other names such as 'miracles' or 'the Will of Allah'. Just as in those other religions, it is not possible to attempt Pagan magic without having a belief first, as the two are interconnected.

Further Resources

This book includes sources of further information that I think are both relevant to the topic and suitable for someone exploring Paganism. You will find them listed in Chapter 17 under their chapter headings. Also contained at the back of the book is a glossary of the terms used in connection with the various paths.

Things to do

- Why not visit a library and find out the origins of your own surname? It could give a clue to your family origins, either in terms of geographic location or the trade followed.

- Consider the Three Principles of the Pagan Federation. Do they make sense to you? (Remember, they are principles, not rules, and may be interpreted in different ways according to an individual's conscience.)

- If you accept that worship can be achieved by being environmentally friendly, what can you do personally to aid nature? It could be by recycling, supporting a conservation project or any of the other ways mentioned. There are some other ideas in Chapter 2, Sacred Sites.

References

[1] Chthonic means of the earth or underworld.

[2] Of course it is very useful that the Church recorded these practices, because it gives us modern Pagans some ideas of how to emulate our ancestors! Theodor of Canterbury wrote of imposing a three-year penance for disguising oneself as a bull or stag on the Kalends of January in about 690 CE. The tenth-century *Canons of Pelfric* forbids singing heathen songs at funerals. Over 300 years after Theodor, in about 1002 CE, Wulfstan the Archbishop of York prohibited worship of idols, wells, Sun, Moon, fire and water. His pleas were obviously ignored by some as various bishops were still denouncing well worship in around 1238. This goes to demonstrate how Christian conversion was not absolute, and Pagan practices have continued to reappear up until our present day.

[3] The comprehensive and definitive work on this subject is *A History of Pagan Europe* (Jones and Pennick, 1995).

[4] Many Pagans have become interested in finding the derivations of local place names, which may give a clue to the original settlers. For example, -*ton* in a place name frequently means that it was once a Saxon farmstead. Similarly names ending in -*by* are frequently of Norse origin, since that was their word for a town. By seeking out the names of specific locations, one can sometimes find original Pagan sites, such as Harrow-on-the-Hill, which is believed to have derived its name from *hearg* and *harrow*, both meaning a Heathen altar. Some places even contain a God's name, such as Thundersley, which is believed to have been derived from Thunor, a God of the Saxons.

[5] One of the few realistic defining measurements is to discover whether a tribe's language is Brythonic, that is, related to the older forms of Welsh, Breton and Cornish. Having neatly dodged the arguments of historians, we then exchange

them for the even more convoluted debates regarding etymology, pronunciation shift and the original derivation of words.

[6] People believing in a range or pantheon of Gods and Goddesses that they identify with natural forces are sometimes known as Pantheists, as opposed to Monotheists (*mono* = one, *theist* = divinity), who only believe in one God. Pantheism (*pan* = all, *theism* = divinity) sees the Gods' spirit in the entire natural world, which is a similar concept to animism. Animism sees a divine spark in each animal, rock and plant, but those who maintain that a supernatural force only inhabits some of them, a part of the time, are termed Polytheists (*poly* = many, *theist* = divinity).

[7] To further complicate matters, some Pagans see the Goddess as a trinity: Maiden, Mother and Crone, representing the three life stages of womankind and nature in general.

[8] A moot is a regular social meeting of Pagans, in a bar or in someone's house, for the purpose of discussing or being taught about aspects of spirituality.

Chapter 1
Festivals and Rites of Passage

Season of mists and mellow fruitfulness,
Close bosom friend of the maturing sun . . .
(John Keats – 'Ode to Autumn')

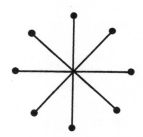

Rites of Passage

Wiccaning

Like most religions, Paganism has its own forms of marking the various stages in life. Practices will vary from path to path, but with many similarities. When a baby is born to a Pagan couple, it is very often presented to the Moon and/or Gods and Goddesses as a sort of introduction to the natural world. The parents may also ask for the help and protection of the five elements – earth, air, fire, water and spirit. This differs from a christening, in that it does not imply that the baby is to be a Pagan, only that protection for it is sought from the deities. It is also an opportunity to introduce the baby to members of your spiritual group, who in many cases may have given spiritual, magical and practical support during the pregnancy. Within Wicca, this ritual is sometimes referred to as 'Wiccaning the Baby', while other traditions may term it the 'Baby Naming'.

In many cultures, great importance is placed upon the knowledge of names (including secret ones not told to outsiders). After all, when we can name something (such as learning technical terms and jargon in a new job), we have power over it, so it is important that others cannot harm magically by being able to give a true, inner name. Consequently some parents will create an additional secret name for the baby, which it will be told about much later in life, either at puberty or on reaching 18 or 21 years of age.

Whether to introduce children to some aspects of Paganism before they are 18 is a hotly contested issue. Some Pagans believe that they should have no teaching at all, and not be asked to make any choices until they are mature enough to do so. Others argue that they are likely to be subjected to other religious pressures before they are 18, and will need the facts about all the faiths so that they can make a balanced decision. Some Pagan parents involve their children in minor ways, or provide special activities for them of a Pagan orientation, such as story-telling, acting out myths, nature walks, etc. Of course, some youngsters bypass their parents completely and find their own path independently. Many Pagan parents are pleased when, in what has become a mainly secular world, their children take an interest in any religion, even if it is not their own. I count myself among them, with a daughter I am proud of at a Christian theological college.

Puberty

Adolescence is always an important time in a young person's development, as ideals and ideas acquired then often last a lifetime. Some Pagan families will make a special celebration of a daughter's first menstruation, so that it can be acknowledged as a healthy, positive gift, rather than have the taboo status afforded it elsewhere. This may be conducted by just the female members of the family, or may include close male family members also. Not many Pagan families seem to mark the coming to manhood of their sons with such importance, although there are individual and notable exceptions.

Initiation

Some Pagan groups demand that initiation be gone through for individuals joining them. This can be anything from taking an oath of secrecy and loyalty through to experiencing a number of 'ordeals'. There may be further stages of initiation as the individual progresses through degrees of status. For example, Gardnerian Witches have three degrees, each with their attendant rituals. In some Wiccan paths initiation is by a sexual encounter with the initiating priest or priestess. Nowadays this is the exception rather than the rule, and only tends to be used when the initiator is already the initiate's established sexual partner. In other cases a symbolic coupling is substituted, such as the *athame* knife being plunged into the chalice cup.

Many groups keep their initiation rites secret, so that the candidate experiences them without any preconceived notions. Some initiations simply involve questions being asked, for which the candidate must respond with an approved answer. Some follow ancient example by requiring the candidate to bathe beforehand as a ritual form of cleansing, and to put on new clothes or a robe at some stage to symbolise their rebirth. Preparation through quiet meditation and fasting is also sometimes required. Some rites involve loosely binding the hands or feet, with the cord being undone at the end to signify the new freedom the path brings, unfettered by previous experiences. Many initiation rituals involve a physical introduction of the candidate to the various elements, and a blindfold may be used during part of this to heighten the experience. Thus you may be expected to plunge your hand into some earth or water, or feel the heat of a flame and air being moved by a fan. Some groups take this further by, for examples making the introduction to earth by having the candidate enter a cave, and to water by having them enter a pool or waterfall. In this way the candidate truly experiences the full force of the elements.

All these forms of initiation have in common an important principle: initiation is a transformation process within the individual, which may happen or not, regardless of how elaborate or brilliantly executed the initiation ritual is. When such a process occurs, the initiation is said to have 'taken'. Initiation is often referred to as a form of rebirth, and some people take on new names to signify this. Some groups will get the initiate to crawl through a tunnel of legs, mimicking the birth process. Others may lead the candidate through a ritual, at the end of which they are promised a glimpse of a divine being. They inevitably do get such a glimpse, when they are eventually shown a mirror. Initiation is a very powerful personal process, and the feeling of joy and exhilaration when it is successfully completed is often the starting point for an extended party.

Self-dedication and Initiation

Some groups do not expect, or even believe in, initiation, but may approve of what is called a 'dedication'. Some solo practitioners also make a personal dedication for themselves as well, or may decide to make a dedication that will apply until such time as they can find a group with which to work. Personal dedications vary greatly, but most often contain elements of rejecting one's past and starting anew, committing to a particular path and declaring oneself to be a Witch, Pagan, Shaman or whatever. Sometimes the dedication may include a promise to obey a set of ethical rules, or to devote oneself to a certain God or Goddess. Anybody can do this; remember, it is you and only you who can truly decide what you are, and nobody can legitimately deny you this right. Thus if you declare yourself a Pagan or a Witch or whatever, you are one by your own definition. I quote below an example of a typical self-dedication.

> I do solemnly declare, before all of the Gods and Goddesses, and my Ancestors, that I dedicate myself as a Pagan and a Witch. I cast off my former life and stand naked and reborn. I commit myself to studying and experiencing the path of Wicca, and promise the deities and myself that I will never misuse the knowledge and power I may gain. I ask for the help of the Lord and Lady, and ask them to witness the start of my new life and the taking of a new name, 'Moonchild' – Blessed Be!'[1]

Some Wiccan paths recognise that it is often difficult for an individual to find someone to initiate them, and therefore prescribe written rites of self-initiation. This has caused much controversy in the past, with many Witches saying you can only become a Witch by being initiated by one of the opposite sex who has themself been properly initiated. Many have refused to recognise the legitimacy of self-initiation or dedication, although attitudes have relaxed in recent years.

Handfasting

Pagan marriage is usually called 'handfasting'. The term comes from the practice of loosely tying the wrists of the bride and groom together before they jump over a broomstick, candle or fire. No 'father of the bride' role is usually taken, since Pagans do not consider a woman can be 'given' away. The words of each ceremony will be very different, and often will be composed solely for that rite. It is common for the couple to formulate their own vows. These may be set to last for a year and a day, for life, for eternity, or so long as love shall last.

The aspect of renewing one's marriage each year has its benefits as well as its drawbacks. It reminds couples not to take each other for granted. I once met a couple from Yorkshire who had been together for many years. I asked the wife, who was very down to earth and blunt, whether they had got handfasted for life or renewed their vows each year. 'Nay, lad,' she winked, 'year and a day's better – at least the old devil takes me out for a meal once a year to propose!'

A handfasting is often when non-Pagan friends and family experience the couple's religion for the first time. Many may be slightly apprehensive to begin with, and it is always heartening to hear the many positive comments of people afterwards, saying how meaningful and unique the ceremony was in being so personalised to the celebrants.

Pagan weddings are not legally recognised in the UK, so some Pagans also have a Register Office ceremony. However, in Iceland and in some States of the USA, the Pagan ceremony carries full legal rights.

Funerals

At one time, the modern Pagan movement was of an age group that did not have to contemplate funerals very often, but with the maturing of those who came into it in the 1950s and 1960s, this has become more of an issue. Pagan funerals are as diverse as any other group's practices. They may be burials or cremations, and they are often very individualistic, with instructions left by the deceased in their will as to a favoured form or the music to be used.

An increase in natural burial grounds (where coffins are replaced with eco-friendly willow baskets and headstones by tree planting) has encouraged many to arrange their final rites in that manner. Some people choose to be buried on their own land, which is permitted under UK law with certain provisos.

Sometimes during a funeral rite a 'talking stick' (which can be a wand or an ordinary piece of wood) is passed from person to person to enable each to have an opportunity to speak about the deceased. Of course, there is sadness and regret, but there is often an air of celebration too, as friends remember the good times, and reflect on the common Pagan belief that death is just another stage of life – a new adventure. Many paths have a psychopomp character within their mythology – a figure that forewarns death, and whose very existence may indicate a tradition's views on fate and death.

There is often talk of returning the elements (water, fire, earth, air and spirit) back to the earth so that they can be reused again, in another life form. Many Pagans also believe in reincarnation, that is, the soul eventually returning in another body. Some Pagans specifically will a sum of money to enable their friends to have a party in their honour, which is similar to the idea of an Irish wake.

Although Pagans belonging to a specific group will often have their funeral conducted by a fellow member, those who follow a solitary path have had problems with organising ceremonies such as funerals and handfastings to their liking. This has been solved in the UK by an organisation called LifeRites, which supplies recommended celebrants for alternative forms of rites of passage. It also offers advice and training. (See Chapter 17, page 182, for details.)

It is a good idea to make it clear in your will what sort of funeral is wanted, in case something inappropriate is provided. For example, you may want to make sure that your Pagan friends are invited, or you may wish to provide contact details for a 'green' burial site. It might all sound a bit morbid, but personally I found it quite liberating to write my own funeral ritual, choose the music, and so on. Death should hold no fears for the Pagan, as most of us regard it as another part of life. Those of the Northern Tradition have both a family and a warrior heaven to choose from. Many Pagans also believe in reincarnation:

> Pagans can have no idea what will happen to them when they die and what the process of reincarnation will be. The general belief among Pagans is in the concept of a period of rest after death followed by conscious preparation for physical rebirth. The Celts saw the after world, which they called The Summerlands, as a reality and not a place of dread to be feared. (Kemp, 1993)

Seasonal Celebrations

Like many other religious paths, Paganism has a set of seasonal festivals. Ours tend to be closely related to the cycles of the natural world, but may also include specific commemorations of past events. Each path will have its own calendar, but many Pagans celebrate the Celtic-derived Eightfold Wheel of the Year, whether or not they follow a specifically Celtic path. There is even doubt as to whether what has been popularly termed 'Celtic' is in fact Anglo-Saxon or Germanic:

> The historic sources clearly demonstrate that Yule, Lent, Easter, Summer, Midsummer, Harvest, Winter and Midwinter all derive from the language of the Anglo-Saxons. Furthermore, these names are found throughout the Germanic language group, in countries such as Sweden and Denmark that have never been inhabited by Celtic language speakers. This would suggest that the major divisions of the English traditional year are of Anglo-Saxon rather than Celtic origin. These survivals from the Anglo-Saxon year must surely have provided the fabric into which later traditions, such as May Day and Halloween, have been woven. Future research could usefully re-examine received wisdom about the origins of English folk customs, many of which are assumed to have Celtic origins, but are not found in the Celtic regions of Britain or Ireland. (Sermon, 2001)

From this it would seem quite appropriate for non-Celtic paths to use what has always been thought to be a Celtic practice.

> The rituals of the eight solar holidays, the Sabbats, are derived from the myth of the Wheel of the Year. The Goddess reveals Her threefold aspects: as Maiden, She is the virgin patroness of birth and initiation; as Nymph, She is the sexual temptress, lover, siren, seductress; as Crone, She is the dark face of life, which demands death and sacrifice. The God is son, brother, lover, who becomes his own father: the eternal sacrifice eternally reborn into new life. (Starhawk, 1979)

Research by Ron Hutton and others has shown that some societies did not celebrate all eight festivals, and two of them may have been added at a later date to provide an equal division of the year. The dates quoted for each festival are only approximate, due to the solar year being out of step with the calendar year. Also, it should be emphasised that since the festivals celebrate natural events, such as the arrival of spring, and so on, some prefer to measure by more natural means that the Christian calendar. Hence the arrival of spring may be acknowledged by the appearance of the first snowdrops, lambs, etc., rather than by a fixed date.

Some Pagans prefer to celebrate the festivals on their original dates. In 1752, Britain and the colonies missed 11 days out of the calendar in order to get it back in line with the earth's solar orbit time of 365.2422 days. Hence Old May day is around 12 May, and Hallowe'en on 11 November, which nowadays is appropriately Remembrance Day, when the UK remembers its war dead. The following correspondences are general, and may vary considerably between individual Pagan beliefs. They are also applicable only to the Northern hemisphere; the Southern hemisphere has its seasons reversed, and so too the natural cycle of vegetation and festivals.

Samhain – October 31

Pronounced *Sow-wain*, this is the start of the Celtic New Year, and the end of the old one. It has been suggested that the name means 'summer's end'. The more recent All Saints Day, and consequently All Hallows Eve, were introduced by the incoming Christian Church. This has resulted in the festival being referred to as Hallowe'en. Inevitably the more ghoulish aspects have been promoted by newspapers and shops, obscuring the sacred meaning. Trick or treating (the playing of practical jokes and begging for sweets) was exported to the USA by European immigrants, where it flourished and developed into a commercialised event, eventually spreading back to its place of origin in an altered form.

Pagans regard Samhain as the time when the veil between this world and the 'other world' is at its thinnest, so remembering ancestors and practising divination are popular at this time. In the old days when not all the cattle could be fed over the winter, the slaughter of some would provide a surplus of meat before the leaner times of winter when food supplies ran low. There are few leaves on the trees at this time, and so the festival came to symbolise the death phase of plants, animals and people.

Yule Solstice – December 21

The winter Solstice is the time for cheering oneself up in the cold miserable days of winter. This is also the New Year for Norse and

Saxon Pagans. Although it is winter, and the longest night, the Sun is reborn and the days start to get longer after this date.

Imbolc – February 2

This festival is sometimes spelt Imbolg, which is more the way it is pronounced, and is also known as Candlemas. At this time the first shoots of early plants are seen, giving a promise of new growth. In human terms this could be seen as pregnancy, and its name is usually seen as referring to ewes' milk.

Spring Equinox – March 21

The length of day and night is now equally balanced. This is the time of the Goddess Eostre who gave her name to the Christian period of Easter.

Beltaine – May 1

The evening before this is known as Walpurgis Night. New life abounds, and many folk customs celebrate the fertility of the land and its people at this time of year. It is also the time of many traditional folk customs such as dancing round maypoles, and creating dancing horses and green men. It is no accident that many mythologies have a Priapic God within their pantheon, i.e. one with a large erect phallus. Beltaine translates as 'bright or good fire', and ritual fires were and are often lit at this time.

Midsummer Solstice – June 21

Sometimes called *Litha*, this is a major date for the Druids, who particularly acknowledge the Sun at its time of maximum strength. The paradox is that this time also signals the weakening of the Sun's power from now on in the cycle. It is also likened to the child maturing into the young man or maiden.

Lughnasagh – August 1

Pronounced *loo-nar-sar*, and sometimes also called Lammas (from Loaf Mass), this is the original time of the corn harvest (and the death of the corn king God) in the days before farmers started sowing more than one crop per year. It represents the time of life when the individual reaches full maturity as a father or mother. Lugh is a Celtic God of light.

Autumn Equinox – September 21

This is sometimes called the Modron Equinox. Day and night are equal in length again, which reminds us of the darker times to come, and of the darker aspects of our deities. It represents the time when we grow old, and take on the Elder's role of giving valued advice and leadership, before dying at Samhain.

Thus we progress through the natural seasons round to Samhain again. Having celebrated so much life, it seems unfair that most outsiders are given a very unbalanced emphasis on our only festival celebrating death. (I use the word 'celebrating' deliberately, since Pagans see death as a part of life's adventure and hence nothing to fear.) These are just a few of the most popular festivals. Wiccans refer to them as *Sabbats*, and to other meetings as *Esbats*. For a complete listing, I would advise consulting the *Tybol Astrological Almanac and Diary*.[2]

Some Pagans meet at the main festivals, others at the Full or New Moons. In common with most ancient practice, the day is considered to start in the evening, and finish at sunset the following night.

Dates of Festivals

Frequently in Pagan and historical books, years will be annotated with BCE or CE. This indicates Before Common Era and Common Era respectively, in preference to the Christian BC and AD (Before Christ and *Anno Domini* – in the Year of Our Lord). However, this event dating is thought to be around four years out. Often festivals were moved to overlay the Pagan ones they were trying to replace. Many Christian churches were built over existing Pagan sacred sites, thus eliminating conflict over where and when to celebrate religious rites.

Nowadays, many Pagans find it most practical to hold celebrations at the weekend nearest to a festival, rather than on the day itself. While a few purists may find this objectionable, most are more concerned with having sufficient time and space to get together without the constraints of going to work the morning after a late-night celebration.

Things to do

- If you have already decided to follow a Pagan path, think about making your own personal dedication in a way that is meaningful for you. If you are not as yet intending to dedicate yourself, consider the implications of doing so – the casting off of old established ways of thinking, a commitment to something very personal and what is sometimes a difficult path, and an uncertain first step into the unknown.

- Go outside. No doubt you know what season it is supposed to be, but pretend you do not. What things indicate the period of the year? It could be the strength of the sun, the growth of a particular plant, or even Hallowe'en goods in shop windows.

References

[1] 'Blessed Be!' is a common exhortation, used throughout Paganism in similar ways as the Christian 'Amen' to signify approval and blessings.
[2] Available from Tybol, 27 Heversham Ave, Fulwood, Preston PR2 9TD, England.

Chapter 2
Sacred Sites

The mysteries these places hold is a metaphor for the ultimate mystery of existence. (Umberto Eco)

What is a Sacred Site?

To a Pagan the whole Earth is sacred, but it is not hard to understand why a stone circle on a wild, windswept moor is seen as being more sacred than a litter-strewn motorway junction. Our Gods and Goddesses are often the personalised essences of individual aspects of nature, which is what gives us a special relationship with it. It should follow that someone who addresses a prayer to a water Goddess is unlikely to want to pollute a river.

You may often hear Pagans talk of the *genius loci*, or spirit of the place. They are referring to the local spirits, ghosts of former inhabitants, elementals or deities. They may also refer to the *Lares*, another Roman term meaning the household Gods. Picking up on atmospheres, whether of the natural world or of human interaction, is a useful skill to acquire. To learn it, one must be prepared to be still, quiet and neutral. It is only then that you can sense what is actually there, rather than reinforce your own preconceived ideas upon the scenario. You must be relaxed and quiet if you want to listen to song-birds. It is even more important if you wish to commune with more ethereal beings. Of course, this is not just a Pagan concept. Lots of people are sensitive to the atmosphere, pleasant or unpleasant, when they visit certain buildings. Many experience a sense of peace and timeless contemplation when they visit an old church, which has been the focal point of prayer for hundreds of years. It is a matter of allowing yourself to use this skill (which we all have to a greater or lesser degree) that is important when you visit special places, approaching them in a quiet, respectful way, and not bringing the chatter and muddled thoughts of the mundane world with you. If you belong to a nature religion, you should be seeking out what the Earth means to you in its natural state:

> The Earth Mother is the most vivid and immediate face which the Goddess presents to us. She is fertility itself, for mankind and for all creatures and plants. She gives birth to us and to them; she nourishes us and them throughout life, and in death receives the empty physical shell back into herself and transforms it into new fertility; for she is both the womb and the tomb, which is again the womb. She maintains the eternal, rhythmic balance by which plant feeds animal and animal feeds plant, and each moreover breathes out the air which the other needs to breathe in. (Farrar, 1996)

It is important for Pagans to have direct experience of nature in the raw, 'red in tooth and claw'. One of the biggest insults that can be made within the Pagan community is to be accused of 'fluffy bunny' Paganism ('Oh look at the cute cuddly creatures, but I do not want to know about them eating each other or the unpleasant looking/acting ones.'). A lion does not think it is being unpleasant when it kills the antelope; it is simply having dinner. Likewise it is important to experience the howling gale or rain while walking across a desolate moor, as well as driving on a bright sunny day to a sheltered place, if you are to truly be in tune with nature. There is no substitute for experiencing nature for yourself, and you cannot class yourself as part of a nature religion if you do not try to experience its power in all its variations. [1]

Of course, there are sometimes restrictions on what you can do if you are disabled or confined to a hospital or prison. Even then, though, you can perhaps open a window and adapt to your circumstances. It may be that you are unable to find a suitable place to celebrate locally. So many woods and beaches are well used by the general public or put out of bounds by private owners. In that case, why not just go out for a walk, before retreating to the privacy of your garden or home for your ritual? Even city dwellers usually have access to a park or other wild corner.

Special Effects

Describing junctions of old crossing places of ancient track ways, Heselton (1995) says:

> Such places, where ancient tracks and paths meet, are still places that witches and other pagans are drawn towards. There is something very magical about such spots, and one can usually find some perfect spot to cast a circle very near the junction but which is protected from view by trees or a hedge. So often have I found such spots that one begins to suspect that they may genuinely have been meeting places going back at least several centuries.

Some stone circles have some peculiar physical properties as well; I have seen compass needles spin wildly in them, which may in some cases be explained by the high quartz content of the stones. As the rocks warm or cool, electric currents are produced, and stored in their rocky batteries waiting to give someone a 'tingle'. You can also get some interesting results by dowsing with rods or pendulums in many such places as well. Another common report from many sites (particularly ancient woods, but also stone alignments) is that time 'stands still' or is otherwise distorted. I have certainly experienced this for myself within a small woodland in Devon. Having been there for what appeared to be no more than an hour or so, on emerging my partner and I found that nearly four hours had elapsed.

Are We Welcome?

Sometimes the spirit of a place may be unwelcoming, and does not want to be disturbed. This may happen if others before you have not treated the location and its inhabitants with respect. In these cases you can either accept the situation and go elsewhere, or try to change it. You may be able to change it by simply saying, 'I come in peace and wish you no harm.'

A more practical option would be to do something positive for the site, such as clearing litter and glass, or wiping off graffiti, thus demonstrating your good intentions. It is always a good idea to carry a litter-bag and protective gloves when visiting such places anyway, since it shows a reverence for nature to leave it better cared for than when you found it.

Occasionally you may experience feelings that a site is not unwelcoming, but seems inappropriate to what you are doing. For example, I once agreed to conduct a male-only ritual at a site unfamiliar to me. When I reached it, the place seemed to exude femininity. On that basis, I changed the location of the ritual, having given thanks to the spirits of the place that they had communicated with me. I do not believe that our very masculine rite would have been successful there. I later went back with a mixed-gender group and on that occasion felt very positive about celebrating there.

Finding Sacred Sites

In the UK we are very fortunate to have many identified sacred sites, from stone circles, stone avenues, man-made hills, mazes, single standing stones and tumuli to those Pagan ritual sites overlaid with the later Christian churches. One should be aware that many of these (including Stonehenge) have been reconstructed by enthusiasts of the last three centuries, with varying degrees of accuracy. 'The two stones flanking the Men-an-Tol (Stone of the Hole) are known to have been moved from their original positions. All three stones are thought to have once formed part of a Neolithic burial chamber' (Bord, 1976).

Some other standing stones have been deliberately destroyed or moved by opponents of the 'Old Religion'. However, somewhat surprisingly many images we may consider Pagan are common inside old churches. I am thinking of the Green Man figure (with foliage issuing from his nose, mouth or ears), the Sheila-na-Gig (a female figure displaying her genitalia) and the Woodwose (the man of the woods, bearing a club). Interest in such figures has grown in recent years, and I have spent many happy hours in old churches looking for them. The definitive study for Green Men has to be that

of Anderson and Hicks (1990). It is also worth checking out whether
there are any mazes accessible within your area. Not all of them are
Pagan-oriented, but it is well worth conducting a meditation while
walking one such as the Saffron Walden turf maze and others like it
as described by Pennick (1990). This book also offers advice on how
to construct the traditional pattern for yourself, should you wish to
add mystery to your garden.

I believe that some particular locations are over-used. It is not
uncommon for more than one Pagan group to turn up at a stone
circle at the same time, especially around the festivals and full Moons.
Although it is good to experience these places (particularly at
less busy times of year), I sometimes think that using some of the
lesser-known sacred wells and trees[2] could provide an answer to the
problem, and would ensure their survival at a time when they may
be under threat. Most areas of the UK and Europe have sacred wells.
Consulting a large-scale local map of your area or researching local
folklore can often locate them. What better way to serve your
Gods and nature (and yourself) than by finding and cleaning up a
neglected sacred site?

Of course, if we as Pagans classify the whole world as a sacred
place, then ideally we should strive to protect all of it. It is our
responsibility, and we cannot leave it to others. As Adrian Harris
(Harvey and Hardman, 1995) of the Dragon Eco Pagan movement
said:

> But despite all the Green rhetoric, nothing has fundamentally changed.
> For most companies 'environmental awareness' means having a Green
> public relations strategy. Government environmental policy is a
> half-baked compromise, motivated by a vote-catching mentality that
> avoids real change. That leads campaigners to concentrate on short-term
> crisis management, trying to slow the destruction of the rainforests,
> or urging reticent governments to patch up the ozone layer. Such
> campaigns tend to be exercises in damage limitation; it is sticking-
> plaster environmentalism, desperately treating the symptoms of the
> environmental crisis, but doing very little to deal with the underlying
> disease.

There is a tendency to rely upon the researches of others to identify
sacred sites, but it is within the capabilities of most people to do this
for themselves, and if a place feels sacred to you personally, then it is.
You may also visit some famous sites that feel 'dead'. It is likely that

they have been disturbed too frequently by people unsympathetic to their purpose, and have thus lost their special energy.

Names of places are often the key to discovering unused but special places. For example, when I moved into my present home, I noticed that there was a Harrow Hill and a Redbeards Wood marked on a large-scale map of the area. 'Harrow' usually derives from the Saxon *hearg* or altar, and 'Redbeard' is a nickname for the God Thor. Sometimes a well or spring will be dedicated to a Christian saint, but many of these reflect a Christianisation of earlier local deities. Thus the Goddess Ellen of the Land often appears in place names as St Helen, and Bride or Brid (of the Brideswell) becomes St Bridget.

Several years ago a friend and I located a 'St Helen's Well' in Norfolk from a map. We spent a hot morning trying to penetrate an overgrown corner of heath and woodlands to find it. Hot, dirty and exhausted, we stumbled into a small clearing. A deer, lying down hidden in the long grass, got up slowly to her feet, stretched and stared us full in the eye. Sedately, she slowly walked away to reveal the wellspring next to where she had been lying. Normally deer try to stay hidden, or panic and crash away through the undergrowth when confronted by humans. You may put whatever interpretation on this event that you like, but we were both profoundly moved by it, and spent the rest of the day clearing old branches and leaves from the wellspring. After a 'thank you' and a drink, we returned to civilisation, changed men. My friend still visits the well regularly and keeps it clean.

One of the other sources of clues as to where sacred sites may exist is the collection of views commonly referred to as 'Earth Mysteries'. Some Pagans have a particular specialist interest in this, including the theory of 'ley lines' suggested by Alfred Watkins in his book *The Old Straight Track* (1974). Watkins proposed that ancient features of the landscape, which form exact alignments, are significant, and that these alignments (or ley lines) have an integral power. Most modern researchers will only accept that an alignment exists where five or more specific old monuments fall in close proximity and exactly on a line drawn on a large-scale map. [3]

TC Lethbridge also provides much food for thought in his books, especially concerning chalk figures cut into hillsides. The Uffington White Horse, the Long Man of Wilmington and the Cerne Abbas Giant can still clearly be seen, while others have become overgrown.

Lethbridge (1957) caused particular controversy when he said he had discovered other hidden figures by probing a rod at close intervals beneath the soil of the Gogmagog Hills outside Cambridge.

Another early writer on earth energies was Straight Track Club member Arthur Lawton. In 1938 he postulated that leys and prehistoric sites marked a network of subtle energy and that this power could be detected. He found the occurrence of certain standard distances and speculated that this was due to a 'cosmic force' creating crystalline patterns on the Earth's surface. (Heselton, 1995)

What Should We Leave?

> A poem, a prayer, laughter, thanks . . . these are all offerings which are appreciated by most sites. A couple of crumbs perhaps that the local birds can eat, a couple of drops of purified water, these things will not cause any problems. What you have to consider is how long that bunch of flowers you're leaving behind will take to biodegrade – and what would happen if everyone who visited each site left behind that amount? (Norfolk, 2001)

It is too easy to attribute litter and other desecration of a site to others. After all, it isn't just Pagans who visit them. I regret to say, though, that in my experience (and in other people's) it is more often people who label themselves Pagans who damage sites, albeit unwittingly or through ignorance. Chalking a symbol onto a wall or dripping candle wax may destroy lichens that have taken thousands of years to grow. Lighting a fire, or burning candles or incense can cause cracking in rocks, and is unsightly as well as leaving harmful ash and soot deposits. Coins, fruit and even water inserted into cracks in rocks will expand, causing them to crack and crumble. Night light containers, dead flowers, food, packaging and cigarette ends will all affect the ambience of the site and annoy the local entities. Cleaning these all up will bring you closer to your gods.

The owners of these sites are, of course, more likely to grant access to those who look after them. In some cases they have appointed local Pagans as official guardians. Some sites, such as the Rollright Stones in Oxfordshire, have associations or trusts that you can support, either financially or practically. You may also be interested in joining larger national organisations, such as English Heritage or the National Trust, who own and manage many important sites. Membership of such organisations frequently allows free or reduced-price admission as well as newsletters and talks. If enough Pagans were vocal in these organisations, we could achieve more sensitivity towards our beliefs concerning the sites they maintain. Access has become a problem in recent years, especially at high-profile locations such as Stonehenge. It has taken a lot of delicate negotiations with the authorities for Pagans to be allowed to celebrate at these sites; this permission could be instantly revoked if litter and vandalism are experienced. Another problem can be the erosion of the soil around sites by the sheer weight of numbers of feet.

From a spiritual point of view, you should also think about how appropriate a rite is for a given location. Invoking Egyptian or Native American deities in the middle of a Celtic monument hardly seems a good idea, and casting (or worse still failing to close) a circle within a sacred space that has already been defined by centuries of use is not honouring the spirit of the place. You can cast a circle any-where, but it is inadvisable to do it in a place where it may clash with existing boundaries and archetypes. As Andy Norfolk (2001) says:

> When creating a circle, most people are imposing an energetic barrier of their own making upon a space. Considering the fact that there is an existing energetic structure at the site already, this is analogous to walk-ing into someone's front room and re-arranging the furniture without asking.

Creating Your Own Sacred Site

The ancient sites were in existence long before us, and if we take care should survive long after us, without us needing to change them in any way. We should only take memories away. Of course, there is no reason why we should not create new sacred sites of our own. Some Pagans groups have done just this, saving up to buy woodland, or in at least one case creating a new, astronomically aligned stone circle.

You could also create a sacred space within your garden, with stones, a pool or even a maze. It is also good if you can include an environment supportive of wildlife, such as a pool for frogs or plants suitable for butterflies to lay eggs on. Not everybody has a garden, but even so you can make a small ritual space or altar within your own household. Choose a quiet, peaceful place not easily seen by visitors, and fill it gradually with objects that are special to you, such as a fir cone from a favourite wood, a pebble from a special beach, or a feather you have found. Add a candle and a container of water and you will have the elements of earth, air, fire and water represented. A picture or statue of your particular deity will represent spirit. Many Pagans do this, and some have several altars dotted around their homes.

Earth Healing

Our contemporary revival of witchcraft and paganism demonstrates not only the collapse of Christianity but our deep need for forms and images that bring living contact, a realization of connection . . . The faery realm is the original pristine world, the nature from which our natural world is devolved, but if we seek to fix our world in some ideal mould we poison it. This may be the ideal mould of scientific manipulation, or the ideal of the utterly natural and unadjusted. (Stewart, 1992)

Some Pagans conduct Earth Healing rituals, in which they back up practical work such as clearing litter with raising energy to restore the wellbeing of the Earth. They may also concentrate their efforts on a specially agreed annual 'Earth Healing Day', while others will say that this should be an all-year-round activity. I have been involved in some Earth Healing Day events and they have always seemed to turn out positively, whatever the size of the gathering or the location. Friendships have been made with council officials and park rangers, pleasantly surprised that a group of people wants to help clean up the place. We have even been in danger of being thought of as 'nice, reasonable people' by those who would have otherwise been very suspicious of us! One man summed it up nicely at the end of a group litter pick and ritual: 'If they suddenly made it illegal to be Pagan again, I guess we have just now given them enough evidence to convict us!'

Other Pagans take the view that nature does not need our spiritual patronage, and has managed very well by itself for centuries, regulating mankind by means of the elemental forces of flood, hurricane, earthquake or fire. This fits in very well with the Gaia[4] theory proposed by James Lovelock, a NASA scientist who found that the Earth had very good self-regulatory systems for sustaining life throughout time. Despite revision of some of his original hypotheses, the idea of treating the Earth as a living, sentient being has caught the imagination of a great number of people, who have continued to spread the theory through various environmental groups and religious paths.

Sacred Landscape

It is now apparent that the ecological pragmatism of the so-called Pagan religions was a great deal more realistic in terms of conservation ethics than the more intellectual monotheistic philosophies of the revealed religions. (HRH Prince Philip, 1990)[5]

If as Pagans we respect the Earth and natural ways of doing things, then we should be endeavouring to extend this respect to our agricultural practices. The last few years have revealed the consequences of using masses of chemicals on intensively farmed soil and feeding and rearing animals in unnatural ways. Diseases and allergies in humans and animals are a direct result of some of these practices. The quality of life of factory farmed animals, confined in dark, small, enclosed places, pumped full of artificial stimulants; the dangers of genetically modified crops; the destruction of natural habitats, from woodlands and hedgerows through to rainforests – all these have become issues for those who care about the way we live and how we interact with natural processes. It is very easy to say 'What difference can I make as one lone individual?' but the fact is, each in our small way we can.

We can refuse to buy GM (genetically modified) and non-organic foods. We can insist on free-range eggs and meat, and timber and paper products from renewable resources. We can purchase goods from local suppliers, travelling there in environmentally friendly transport. By using local suppliers of meat, it is easier to check on the farming methods. You would also be supporting a local economy and preventing cattle from being transported vast distances before being slaughtered, to end up in anonymous supermarkets that may only pay lip service to being sensitive about their sources of products. We can recycle plastic, paper, metal and glass packaging, and show a preference for products that do not waste those materials. We can refuse to buy canned fish from suppliers who do not use dolphin-friendly nets, and boycott products that pollute the atmosphere and destroy the ozone layer. Money is what drives big business. If enough people fail to purchase an environmentally unfriendly product, stores and manufacturers will soon get the message and replace it, whether they want to or not.

If you do not think it can be done, consider the fur trade; what was once the height of luxury fashion is now the socially unaccept-able object of derision. We cannot all be eco-warriors chaining ourselves up to prevent destruction of the environment, although many such people are Pagans, and have had not only direct success with their actions, but the admiration of others through their brave example. That new road might not be necessary if more of us used public transport and voted for politicians who were sensitive to our concerns. And it might be too expensive and politically insensitive to build if enough of us made objections and protests. All these things are a way of showing a love and reverence for nature and its Gods and Goddesses, and are of more practical importance than whatever rituals we do or events we attend.

Many Pagans get on with giving practical help to the natural world in whatever way they can, from financially or physically supporting conservation organisations through to getting involved in projects themselves, such as clean-up campaigns and running animal sanctuaries. In judging whether someone is a Pagan, it is, as they say, more important to see if they 'walk the walk than talk the talk'.

Things to do

- Start recycling at least one material in your household, whether it is paper, glass, plastic or tin, or saving kitchen waste to make into garden compost.

- Choose one environmental campaign to get involved with, whether it be local, national or international.

- When you next visit a special place, take a rubbish bag and protective gloves so that you can bring away some litter with you.

- When you visit a stone circle or similar, take a compass with you and see if anything happens to it, or try dowsing with a pendulum or two pieces of bent coat-hanger wire held lightly in your hands. Mentally tell the dowsing equipment what you are trying to locate, such as a ley line, watercourse or old hidden wall remains. You do not have to be expert or have any experience to succeed.

References

[1] There are types of magic designed for indoor practice, such as Ceremonial and Chaos Magic, both of which are described later, but this is because they are not tied specifically to the Pagan religion, which by its very source demands that we have a close physical affinity to nature. That does not mean that every individual Pagan does frequently go to the great outdoors, but most accept that they should.

[2] Sometimes known as Cloutie or Wishing trees, where people tie cloth strip 'wishes' upon the branches. It is the equivalent of casting a coin into a wishing well.

[3] Most adherents subscribe to a magazine called *The Ley Hunter*, c/o Paul Devereux, PO Box 152, London N10 1EP.

[4] Gaia is a Greek Goddess.

[5] Quoted in *Prediction* magazine, October 1997.

Chapter 3
Hereditary and Traditional Witchcraft

All life is but a wandering to find home.
(Dekker, Ford and Rowley, 1658)

Differences and Similarities

There is more argument, conjecture and disagreement about this particular area of Paganism than any other. In fact, there are many who would argue that Traditional and Hereditary Witches did not (or do not now) necessarily consider themselves Pagan and Wiccan. But first we should try to define what a Traditional or Hereditary Witch actually is, and what they do.

Hereditaries, as suggested by their name, are part of a family line of Witchcraft, to which you can only belong if related by birth or marriage. As society has changed, it has become harder to continue those family ties, which has resulted in some lines dying out. Other Hereditary groups have 'adopted' individuals, whom they trust to continue their tradition. This modern approach has been scorned and derided by some families.

Hereditary practice, where it is known, appears to be very

simplistic and basic, using a few non-metal ritual tools. It has no 'Book of Shadows' (a collection of spells and ceremonies) nor a complicated seasonal calendar of customs. Inevitably it has survived best in rural communities, close to the land, which they venerate. It is almost impossible to say how many such families exist, since they tend to be quite secretive, and are not generally involved with the wider Pagan community. Some even seem to follow a dualistic path, seeing no conflict between going to a Christian church and practising their magic as a complementary activity, and having no feeling of these two religious ways being at odds with each other. Some say their practice is a Craft, rather than a religion, and they simply carry it on because it feels right, without any need for a detailed theology or fancy jargon.

Traditional Witchcraft shares some of these traits, but is distinguished by the fact that it is not exclusive to any one family. It is supposed to have existed for generations before the advent of modern movements in the 1950s. Once again, their rituals tend to be beautiful in their simplicity, with very little ornamentation or paraphernalia, and a greater emphasis on worshipping a Horned God than in more modern Witchcraft rites. The God is sometimes represented by a *stang* (forked stick) within ceremonies, and may sometimes be identified with the Herne the Hunter of Windsor Forest, the Celtic Cernunnos, or the Greek Pan, but is just as likely to be referred to as 'Old Horny', 'the Lord' or 'Him'. Some of these God representations are horned like a goat, others antlered like a deer.

As well as this, both a Dark and Light Goddess are acknowledged, sometimes identified as Arianrhod (as Dark Goddess) and Diana or Bride (as the Goddess of Light or the Moon). These Goddesses are from a variety of cultures and mythologies. More often they are referred to generically as the Goddess or the Lady. (Incidentally, the names of the main pair of Nordic Vanic deities, Frey and Freya, translate as Lord and Lady.) This is in contrast to some modern Witchcraft rites, which tend to shun the darker aspects, and frequently espouse a triple Goddess form of Maiden, Mother and Crone.

In the main, Traditional Witchcraft covens have two types of meeting. An *Esbat* (a term possibly invented by Margaret Murray) is a gathering at a specific phase of the Moon (full or new usually), and will be concerned with general magic. A *Sabbat*, which takes place at one of the eight main festivals, is more of a celebration of a stage in the natural year cycle. However, the two types of event are not mutually exclusive.

A circular sacred space is created for most magical work, generally by walking around it with a sword or *athame* (ritual knife). Witches tend to see the circle as a place within which to focus their activities and magic, whilst ceremonial magicians and mediaeval alchemists saw it as a protective barrier to keep them from the demonic forces they summoned. Often the circle will be nine feet wide, which is just big enough for a small group of people to work closely together. Although referred to as a circle, many consider this working space to be a sphere that extends above and below the ground. In most traditions, this will be followed by a call to the spirits of the four cardinal points of the compass. Many, but not all, start in the East and work round to the North, then reverse this to close the circle at the end of the rite. This is sometimes referred to as 'calling the quarters' or 'erecting the Watchtowers'. Some groups use particular tools or objects to represent the elements at each point. The most popular associations are:

- East – Air, represented by a wand or incense
- South – Fire, represented by a sword
- West – Water, represented by a chalice
- North – Earth, represented by a *pentacle*, which is most often a circular platter with symbols inscribed upon it.

The fifth element of Spirit (corresponding to the top point of the universal pentagram star symbol) is generally located in the centre of the circle.

I would emphasise that there are many different variants of the most popular correspondences I have detailed here, and that many of the practices mentioned here are also carried out by other Pagan groups described in the next few chapters.

When the circle has been opened, Gods and Goddesses will be welcomed to it. It is considered very important that the circle is closed properly at the end, thanking and bidding farewell to the elements and deities. Some groups hold a shared meal of cakes and ale (or other food and drink) before the circle is closed, while others have a more elaborate feast afterwards.

One ritual act that is shared by both traditions is the Drawing Down of the Moon. This rite is a divine mystery, almost impossible to fully encapsulate in words, but involving the priestess or priest inviting the God or Goddess to take possession of their bodies (the God into the priest, and the Goddess into the priestess). The priestess (or priest), assisted by the coven members, will build up a trance state in which they allow themselves to be possessed, and thus act on behalf of the deity.[1] This process has been described as both exhilarating and totally scary – a complete voluntary submission of your personality for a period, during which you are not in control of your own body. It is considered unwise for anybody to attempt this without the correct attitude, preparation or training.

> What they practice is neither exactly a religion, nor is it exactly magic; yet both labels, if applied in their broadest sense, describe something of the way Traditionals function. (Jones and Matthews, 1990)

As with Hereditary Witchcraft, there is certain kudos attached by some to being part of what they see as a pure, continuous historic line. This has been comprehensively challenged by Professor Ronald Hutton in his book *The Triumph of the Moon* (2000). Despite detailed research, Hutton has failed to find any evidence of pre-1950 origins for these groups. Of course, failing to find evidence does not prove that something never existed, and the evidence for something that was illegal and subject to extreme prejudice before 1950 is bound to be scarce, if non-existent. I doubt whether one would find written plans for a 1940s bank robbery either! I respect Ron Hutton's opinions, especially as he has publicly 'come out' as being a Pagan, as well as being a respected academic. However, I would argue with the academic premise that a thing does not exist if it cannot be found in literature. I know from my work in the field of folk traditions that the oral process is far more accurate than it has previously been given credit for, even if it is susceptible to distortion and manipulation. Of course, there will always be individuals who deliberately mislead people into thinking they have some great historical basis upon which they base their beliefs, for example, some Druids and Freemasons, certain Christian sects and even the Nazis! Some groups claiming to be Traditional even appear to have some practices of a modern provenance contained within them. In their defence it has to be said that there is no reason why a Traditional group should not augment their ancient practice with newer material that appeals to them. They may quite genuinely believe they are Traditional themselves, but may possibly be mistaken in how far back their history goes. After all, in 50 years, they may have had five or more generations of Witches handing down what is mainly an oral tradition. The modern members of such groups have been handed down a tradition several generations old, even if it was new in 1950.

One of the few times when Traditional and Hereditary Witches have worked together was during World War Two, when they made a joint magical effort to oppose the Nazis, who were not averse to using occult means themselves. Not only did the British Witches put themselves at magical and physical risk (which reportedly led to the death of two of them), but as the Witchcraft Act was still in force at this time, they could have been arrested and jailed as well.

It is said that several covens in the South of England worked together, either holding rituals at the same time in different places, or in at least one case combining for a joint ritual. This was unusual, since only coven leaders had knowledge of groups in the adjacent area, but it was obviously thought worthwhile to compromise confidentiality and the threat of being found out by the authorities, who were especially vigilant about groups of people meeting in secret during wartime. Reportedly, the Witches danced to a point of exhaustion, repeatedly chanting a phrase designed to deter invasion. This process has been termed 'raising a cone of power', and is reputed to have been used to turn back the Spanish Armada as well.

One English Spiritualist medium, Helen Duncan, was actually jailed in 1944 after making some predictions far too accurate for the authorities' comfort. It has been conjectured that these two events, coupled with the strength of the Spiritualist movement, hastened the repeal of the Witchcraft Act after the war. (It was finally repealed on 12 June 1951.)

Whenever one deals with an historical activity of which little is known, one also runs into the problems of diversification. When a particular fact is known with some degree of certainty, it still only represents the practice at that particular time within that particular set of people, and may have altered the following day. There is always a danger in generalisation, in that one can erroneously say that because there is proof of one specific incident it must be the case in general. The late Aleister Clay-Egerton, writing in *The Cauldron* magazine (November, 1993), said that he was initiated into a Traditional coven in Cheshire in 1943, where they used a nine-fold kiss.[2] Another associated coven in North Wales at that same time used a seven-fold kiss. In many cases covens were not aware of the existence, let alone the practices, of another coven quite nearby, due to the need for secrecy and protection of identities and reputations.

In an effort to keep those two lines of Traditional and Hereditary Witchcraft unaffected by modern trends and developments, both traditions have sought to distance themselves from other paths at times, and have criticised or even been openly hostile to individuals publicising their rites and beliefs. Some practitioners thought it was essential that their beliefs should be publicised to a wider audience, if only to ensure their survival, while others thought that this would destroy the holy mysteries of their Craft (another name for Witchcraft) and would attract the wrong sort of people to it.

It is believed by some that part of the spiritual path of a Witch is the personal quest to find others of a like mind, and that those destined to become Witches are fated to find the right coven through personal effort. This might work in small rural communities, where 'people know people who know people', but is more difficult in modern society. Maybe this highlights the point that Witchcraft is ideally a country pursuit, and less suited to urban culture.

The Pickingill Papers

There have been times when the members of Traditional and Hereditary groups have sought to remedy what they have seen as incorrect information being put out by others. Nowhere is this more evident than in the case of the Pickingill Papers.

George Pickingill was a 'Cunning Man' (that is, a solo village magician), born in 1816 in Canewdon, Essex. He had a fearsome and widespread reputation for magical acts, and was also reputed to be the leader of a group of traditional Witches. He died in 1909, at the ripe old age of 93.[3] The papers named after him were published in the mid- to late 1970s, in two magazines, *The Wiccan* and *The Cauldron*. They were the writings of a man, now living in New

Zealand, who claimed to be a member of Hereditary Craft. His name was EW 'Bill' Liddell, but he also used the pseudonym 'Lugh'. He said that he had been instructed by some of his Elders to act as a conduit for their views, and then proceeded to submit many articles, some of which he said he disagreed with, and some of which were not consistent in approach with previous ones. The accuracy and origins of these papers have been the source of much heated debate ever since, and were the subject of a concerted public attack by the writer Aiden Kelly. As Professor Ronald Hutton has pointed out, considering the wide range of contacts Pickingill was supposed to have, it is surprising that there are no other corroborating documents written by any of those contacts. Pickingill seems have been exalted by the likes of the writer Eric Maple[4] to back up their own claims to fame.

Some saw the papers as an attack on modern Wicca (a general name attached to modern Witchcraft traditions)[5], while others saw them as confirmation that Wicca's origins had a sound historical basis rather than being mainly a twentieth-century invention. Certainly the papers painted a very different picture to that of the feminine-inspired paths, with a 'Man in Black', or Magister (a Latin term for teacher), acting as the leader of the group, or even of several groups of Witches. However, there were counter-claims that other groups did allow female Magisters. The papers also alleged that Murrell (who was regarded as a bit of a renegade by other Traditional/Hereditary Craft practitioners) was a direct influence on both Aleister Crowley and the Hermetic Order of the Golden Dawn, and that the notable occultist Austin Osman Spare (1888–1956) was a member of an Essex coven run by a Mrs Paterson. It also said that the New Forest coven, so important in the origins of Gardnerian Witchcraft (see Chapter 4), was connected to Pickingill's Nine Covens.

The papers also point to Hereditary and Traditional Witchcraft as surviving most strongly in my native East Anglia (also a stronghold of the all-male Horse Whisperers magical guilds), as well as Sussex, Hertfordshire and Hampshire. That is something I can confirm from my personal experience, yet despite my knowledge and prominence of position within the area, this grouping's almost obsessive secrecy means I have only ever caught the most elusive wisps of evidence of it.[6]

The papers also refer to two rites of induction into Hereditary Craft, which I have had confirmed independently elsewhere as existing within some groups. These inductions are of a sexual nature, male passing power to female and vice versa. That initiatory process is a very different thing to the three hierarchical degrees of Gardnerian Wicca (see Chapter 4). Having said that, I understand that some other covens do have some variants to the system. There are also several theories expounded on the connections between Traditional Witchcraft and Freemasonry rituals and symbolism. Essentially, such groups are very insular, concerned with the well-being of the village and the success of the surrounding agriculture, with no desire to operate in any wider context than that.

Other Sources of Information

Apart from the Pickingill Papers, there are two other important sources of first-hand experience of pre-1950s regional Witchcraft. Rhiannon Ryall (1999) gives a very singular view of what it was like to be part of an isolated West Country village coven in the 1940s, celebrating five festivals and acknowledging 'Old Horny' and the 'Green Lady'. She mentions two initiatory levels, and the taking of a person's measure in red thread.[7] She also states that the Great Rite was used as initiation at the second level, and the Drawing Down the Moon ritual (invoking the Goddess into the priestess) could only be performed by those who had gone through it. The Great Rite is sacred sexual intercourse between a male and female Witch. (It also occurs in some other paths.) Rhiannon's group used a specially made metal *athame* ritual knife, as well as a wand, goblet and dishes for salt and cakes, and worked in robes. Although she has had her detractors, I find her eminently more believable than Sybil Leek, who courted the media outrageously with her lurid descriptions of what she claimed was a long Hereditary Craft line, before moving to America.

The Secrets of East Anglian Magic by Nigel Pennick (1995) gives a broad view of East Anglian practices, including Cunning Men, Witches, Horse Whisperers and Toad Witches. Cunning Men acted as village magicians and healers, but sometimes doubled up as the leading male representative for covens of female Witches. The secre-

tive Horse Whisperers' guilds, which seemed mainly to exist from
East Anglia through to the east coast of Scotland, were formed to
pass on methods for training and healing horses. The position of
horseman was considered an elite one by agricultural labourers, and
jealously guarded its secrets. Very little is known about the East
Anglian rites of the Toad Witches, other than they worked magic by
means of some ritually prepared toad bones.

Further afield, giving a useful comparison to the UK, are the
practices of the Italian *Strega* Witches, as detailed in *Aradia, or the
Gospel of the Witches* (1991) by the American folklorist and political
radical Charles Leland in 1886. I understand some of that material is
still used by Italian-American Witches, although I am uncertain
whether the tradition has survived the overpowering Catholicism of
its homeland. This text gives us the term 'Old Religion' and provides
the basis for 'The Charge of the Goddess', which has been adapted
since for modern usage.

If seeking a wider understanding of what Witchcraft was like
nationally pre-1950s, one is invariably drawn to two sources of
information, neither of which can be taken at their face value, the
work of academic folklorists Margaret Murray and James Frazer,
and the records of Witchcraft trials.

Dr Margaret Murray made her name in the early 1920s by
publishing a theory that all the Pagan religions of the ancient world
were closely related aspects of one universal Goddess religion. She
identified the modern-day Witches as being direct descendants of
this continuing Goddess religion. As well as writing her own books,
as President of the Folklore Society she added extra credibility to
Gardner's *Witchcraft Today* when she wrote the foreword in 1954.
Her arguments convinced many people, including many of the
academics of her day, and one can still find her views recycled today.
She advanced some bizarre connections, and it has been proved that
she only used the data she gathered which confirmed her theories,
whilst discarding and hiding that which did not. She has been fairly
well discredited in most modern sources.

Sir James G Frazer (1936), on the other hand, presented a great
wealth of folkloric practice and superstition from around the world
in clear and honest detail in *The Golden Bough*. It makes a fascinat-
ing, if somewhat lengthy read, and if you are only mildly interested
I would recommend the less daunting paperback compilation

instead of the full 13 volumes. Frazer tried to connect all his data to prove his theory that almost all Pagan religious rites were connected to one particular rite of a priest being murdered by his successor in a sacred bower, which most people think unlikely.

The Witchcraft trial records, and the many books that have been compiled from their details, provide the other main source of information on historical Witches. There are also the gruesome and horrifying details of the Witch-hunts of the sixteenth and seventeenth centuries. Some books, notably that of the Catholic priest Montague Summers (1925), are rabidly anti-Witch, although they do still contain interesting material. Once again though, one has to treat the material with suspicion.

Looking at the trial records first, we find alleged confessions of cursing, consorting with the Devil and his familiars, orgies and demonic pacts, as well as flying on broomsticks and all manner of other fantastic material. It would be a very gullible person who believed all this so called 'evidence' en masse. Even the mediaeval courts did not fall for all of them, and there were more accused Witches acquitted than is generally appreciated. For example, four out of the eight people brought from Ipswich to the Bury St Edmunds, Suffolk, England, court in 1645 by the Witchfinder General Matthew Hopkins were acquitted, while the other four were hanged. Hopkins' methods for extracting confessions included keeping prisoners awake for several days and nights, subjecting them to constant hostile questioning and pricking them with pins to find a Witch mark.[8] On occasions the poor victims were also tied up and 'swum' in a pond to establish guilt. Small wonder then that many of the confessions sound remarkably similar! Most people would be pleased to admit to anything the inquisitor wanted, however preposterous, just to stop the torture, regardless whether they were a Witch or not. (Probably many were not. It is noticeable that a fair proportion of the accused where actively disliked by their communities, and often were living on Parish Relief or other charity before they were accused.) Hopkins was a failed lawyer who found a highly profitable niche for himself in a time of great uncertainty and Civil War. He was almost certainly in league with the Parliamentarians, who used his network of paid informers to spy on suspected Royalists. In less than two years he was probably responsible for around 400 executions within East Anglia.

Ophidian Tradition

I have recently come across an obscure movement called Ophidian Traditional Witchcraft, which has been publicised by the author Tony Steele (1998 and 2001). He also calls it Water Witches, in honour of the element they venerate beyond others as a manifestation of the World Serpent. He claims it draws upon an ancient text called the *Oera Linda Book*, compiled over several generations, and was mainly family-based until the 1940s. In 1985 Steele formed an organisation called the *Ordo Anno Mundi*, which has six initiatory degrees and operates in both the UK and USA to further its expansion.

> The two words that sum up the Ophidian view of reality are animism and polytheism.[9] Literally everything is alive, with its own sentience and feelings. Nature abounds with spirits of every kind, many of which are powerful enough to be classed as deities, either Gods or Goddesses (or sometimes androgynous). Ophidians see all Gods and Goddesses as individuals, and do not conflate them together as 'aspects' of each other. They venerate the Mother Earth (called Irtha in the Oera Linda Book) as the most powerful of the Goddesses, mother of all the others. They also of course venerate the World Serpent (Wr-alda) who fertilises Mother Earth with his life-force. Together the World Serpent and Mother Earth brought forth three daughters (Lyda, Finda and Frya), the mothers of the human race. In addition, there is the Horned God (Fosite or Wodin), who is seen as a messenger of the World Serpent. (Tony Steele, Witchvox Web site.)

Ophidians are said to venerate ancestors and to believe in a system of afterlife as well as reincarnation. Their priestesses (they do not have priests) are termed *femmes*, derived from the Frisian term for familiars, and celebrate festivals to a lunar calendar. Their rights and duties are described in detail in *Oera Linda*. Magic is performed by creating a non-physical entity, within a ritual space known as a mill. This consists of three concentric squares.

Traditional Witchcraft in the USA

Inevitably the settlers from many parts of the world took elements of their historic native traditions with them to their new home in

America, to augment the many and varied Native American Pagan traditions. Whether one views the Witch-trial events in Salem, Massachusetts as mass hysteria, a genuine outbreak of European-influenced Witchcraft or, as one convincing study has shown, the reactions of a people unfamiliar with ergot poisoning, certainly they were as aware of Witchcraft as Matthew Hopkins in seventeenth-century England.

Thus the slaves kept alive traditions from Africa, the Italian *Strega* Tradition has been kept going, and so on. Twentieth-century Americans have both brought relatively modern paths such as Gardnerian Wicca to the USA, as well as individuals such as Buckland and Starhawk developing their own forms of Witchcraft. However, one European tradition has survived there, while seemingly dying out at home, and that is the *Hexancrafte* of the Netherlands. Modern-day Dutch Witches tend to follow British or American paths, yet their own home-grown tradition continues to flourish in a small way in Dutch-settled areas of the USA such as Pennsylvania. I understand that some vestiges of Pagan/Witch practices survived within the remote and insular settlements of the Appalachian Mountain area, although little has been published about it to my knowledge.

There is also a group called the New England Covens of Traditional Witches (NECTW), which was founded by Gwen Thompson (1928–86), who claimed a Hereditary line from her grandmother Adriana Porter, who herself died in 1946. Although Gwen believed that practitioners of Witchcraft should remain discreet and underground, she was moved to publish her tradition's version of the 'Wiccan Rede' in *The Green Egg* magazine in 1975 to clear up confusion over it. One of the anomalies of such documents is that they refer to Wicca, but indicate that they are of pre-modern Wicca origins. Confusion sometimes occurs over how the term 'Wicca' is applied. To some it is those strands of Witchcraft originating after 1950, such as Gardnerian, Alexandrian, etc. To others it is inclusive of every branch of Witchcraft. Others exclude solo practitioners from the term. There is no one definition.

The Wiccan Rede document has been much copied since (frequently without giving a source) and I quote it here fully as an example of a set of Hereditary beliefs:

Rede of the Wiccae – Counsel of the Wise Ones

1. Bide the Wiccan laws ye must in perfect love and perfect trust.
2. Live and let live – fairly take an fairly give.
3. Cast the Circle thrice about to keep all evil spirits out.
4. To bind the spell every time, let the spell be spake in rhyme.
5. Soft of eye and light of touch – speak little, listen much.
6. Deosil go by the waxing Moon – sing and dance the Wiccan rune.
7. Widdershins go when Moon doth wane, an the Werewolf howls by dread Wolfsbane.
8. When the Lady's Moon is new, kiss the hand to her times two.
9. When the Moon rides at her peak, then your heart's desire seek.
10. Heed the Northwind's mighty gale – lock the door and drop the sail.
11. When the wind comes from the South, love will kiss thee on the mouth.
12. When the wind blows from the East, expect the new and set the feast.
13. When the West wind blows o'er thee, departed spirits restless be.
14. Nine woods in the Cauldron go – burn them quick and burn them slow.
15. Elder be ye Lady's tree – burn it not or cursed ye'll be.
16. When the Wheel begins to turn – let the Beltane fires burn.
17. When the Wheel has turned a Yule, light the Log an let Pan rule.
18. Heed ye flower, bush an tree – by the Lady blessed be.
19. Where the rippling waters go, cast not a stone an truth ye'll know.
20. When ye have need, hearken not to others' greed.
21. With the fool no season spend or be counted as his friend.
22. Merry meet an merry part – bright the cheeks an warm the heart.
23. Mind the Threefold Law ye should – three times bad an three times good.
24. When misfortune is enow, wear the blue star on thy brow.
25. True in love ever be unless thy lover's false to thee.
26. Eight words the Wiccan Rede fulfil – an it harm none, do what ye will.

Pagan ethics are talked about in detail elsewhere in the book, but the elements of the Threefold Law (believing good or bad actions or spells will be returned three times) in line 23, and the final line 26 (often taken as guiding principle in isolation from the others) are important features. *Deosil* in line 6 means sunwise, or clockwise, and similarly *widdershins* in line 7 means anti-clockwise.

Conclusion

Traditional and Hereditary groups are difficult, if not impossible, to find. Their claims to sources of great antiquity must be viewed with some caution, even though their beliefs may be entirely genuine. If intending to pursue this path, you should question your motives, as you should for every other path. Is it that you want to get as close to historical sources as feasibly possible for their own merit, or do you expect some extra kudos to attach to your choice? Why should that be important to you? I would emphasise, both for these and other traditions, that just because a thing is old, it does not make it necessarily right or appropriate for today. It is quite possible for new ideas to have merit too.

Things to do

- Consider how you feel about an initiation involving sexual intercourse. Would this be something (given the right people and conditions) you would be prepared to go through with?

- You can experience partly what it feels like to be Drawing Down the Moon in the following exercise. You need to find another person you can trust to perform it with you. Agree a time limit (say 10 to 15 minutes) and then promise to say or do whatever they tell you without question or hesitation. If they say move your arm above your head, or tell you to say, 'I am an idiot,' simply do it. After the time is up, see how comfortable you feel about being totally controlled by another power. How far would you personally let them go without refusing? This also ties in with a requirement made in some Wicca initiations for 'Perfect Love and Perfect Trust', where one is expected to follow the High

Priestess's orders without question, because they love you and have your best interests at heart. If you were asked to lean over backwards until you fell, could you trust a group of friends to catch you? If you have some people you could try this with, this would also be a useful way of finding out whether you could live by such a principle.

References

[1] To encourage possession into someone else is termed invoking. To do it to yourself is called evoking.

[2] This practice is sometimes equated with an Eastern rite of opening or purifying the bodily chakras, or spiritual nodes of a person. 'In Gardnerian Wicca the five fold kiss is applied on the feet, knees, phallus/yoni, breast/nipples and mouth of the candidate.' *The Pickingill Papers* (Liddell and Howard, 1994).

[3] He is not the only Cunning Man recorded as operating in East Anglia within this period. Cunning Murrell lived in Hadleigh, Essex from 1812 to 1860 (when he accurately predicted his own death to the minute), and Old Winter was the Cunning Man of Ipswich from around 1795 through to the mid-1800s. Whether they had any contact with each other is uncertain, although it is known that some Cunning Men formed lodges, and like Pickingill also doubled as the Magister for local groups of Witches.

[4] Maple published some articles concerning witchcraft in Essex in the Folklore Society Journal between 1960 and 1965, as well as a book called *The Dark World of the Witches* (Hale, 1962).

[5] Although the term Wicca is applied by some people exclusively as a label for the newer traditions of Witchcraft such as Gardnerian, Alexandrian and Seax, other writers use the words Wicca and Wiccan to cover all forms of Witchcraft. Popular usage has been for the word to be pronounced the same way as 'wicker', but most academics agree the etymology of the word and its Saxon origins would make the pronunciation 'Witch-ar' more correct. There has been some argument whether its roots are in a word meaning 'wise' or another meaning 'to bend'.'

[6] For example, Lois Bourne, a member of Gardner's Brickett Wood coven, has stated (1998) that she was also initiated into a Norfolk Traditional coven by fellow member Monica English. I also know that at least one member of a meeting held in the late 1960s to form what eventually became The Pagan Federation was said to come from a Traditional coven in the Walsingham area of Norfolk. Whether those two covens are the same or separate, or whether they actually were Traditional path, is impossible to say for certain now. I do not even know if either of them was one of the original nine allegedly controlled by Pickingill. I believe I know of the original existence, surviving until 50 years ago (but sometimes more recently), of at least five other groups in East Anglia, but they were all very secretive, and have either died out or managed to hide themselves really well. I believe the low level of Traditional or Hereditary Craft identification in East Anglia is likely to be reflected elsewhere across the UK.

[7] This is common to many paths of Witchcraft. The novice lies on the ground and a red thread is laid around their outline and tied. It is then kept by the Elders, giving a deeper meaning to the phrase 'I've got your measure.' By its means it was believed that the coven could control the individual's actions, and ensure their loyalty and secrecy. Rhiannon Ryall says it was handed back to her after a second initiation, but this is not the case in some other paths. She also notes that hair and nail clippings were taken.

[8] 'Witch marks' were believed to be the teat that is used to suckle a witch's familiar imp or animal. If a mole or wart were found on the body, it might be identified as such. Alternatively, the person could be pricked all over in order to find a concealed Witch mark. It was said these marks had no sensitivity, so if you pricked them no pain would be felt. Consequently, if the victim failed to cry out on the umpteenth time they were pricked, this was taken as evidence against them. I have heard, but cannot substantiate, claims that at least one pricker was made with a retractable point, for times when the victim was being uncooperative.

[9] Animism is a belief that all natural things have the same spark of the divine within them, including rocks, trees and animals. Pantheism is similar, but acknowledges that there can be a whole pantheon of separate gods and goddesses representing different elements of that one divine spark of the natural universe. Following on from that is the belief that as humans have that divine spark within them, it is possible for us to become as gods and goddesses ourselves. Polytheism recognises that there can be several sets of divinities working in parallel.

Chapter 4
Gardnerian Witchcraft

Nor do we suggest that the Gardnerian body of rituals is 'better' than other Wiccan systems. What we do suggest is that, for us and thousands of others, it works.
(Janet and Stewart Farrar, 1990)

Origins

Gerald Brosseau Gardner (1884–1964) is probably unique in the history of British spirituality. In the 1950s he started a religious movement which has since been exported around the world, whereas almost every other religious expression in the UK has been brought here from elsewhere. As a retired colonial customs officer returned from Malaya, with an interest in knives, allegedly masochistic sex and naturism, Gardner seems an unlikely candidate to launch a religious movement. Gardner's life has been re-examined many times, and yet there is still some mystery about this controversial figure. Regardless of his frequent exaggerations and what sometimes appear to be downright lies, he managed to be in the right place at the right time to rally closet Pagans and explore the new-found freedom of religious expression that followed the repeal of the Witchcraft Act in 1951. In doing so, Gardner laid the foundations of what is probably the most popular single persuasion of Witchcraft practised in the West today. His thinking has often influenced even those Witches who do not follow his path, and despite his many faults he remains the Father of Modern Witchcraft. In the introduction to his excellently researched book *Wiccan Roots*, Philip Heselton (2000) observes:

> . . . Paganism is a religion that you don't have to teach. Unlike Christianity, Judaism or Islam, which would cease to exist if all knowledge of them disappeared from the world, paganism would regenerate spontaneously because its roots lie in the depth of each individual and their relationship to the earth and not in any outward teaching.

Of course, such a prominent figure was bound to have many detractors. Some members of the Hereditary and Traditional paths regarded him as a heretic in publicising what was to them a closely guarded secret, and changing many aspects of what they saw as 'correct' practice. Some of the criticisms levelled against him would seem quite minor considerations to the outsider (such as taking metal knives into a ritual), but such actions struck at the heart of what many claimed to have been the orthodox way of doing things for centuries.[1] Some people who initially worked with him later broke away and repudiated some of his claims with inside knowledge. One of these was the late and much-loved Doreen Valiente. It is noticeable that, like many others, she ended up disagreeing with him, but nevertheless found him completely charming and retained a respect for him. He certainly knew most of the major occultists of his day.[2] How much each one influenced him, wrote rituals for him or vouched for his Craft authenticity has kept many publishers in business for years. I do not want to add to that, however, since this book is more focused on what each particular path does or thinks today.

Initiation

Gerald's critics would have found it easier to discredit him if it were not for the fact that he claimed to have been initiated into a New Forest coven in 1939 (subsequently associated with a lady called Dorothy Clutterbuck, but more likely to be a lady known as Dafo according to both Philip Heselton and Ron Hutton).[3] This was generally accepted by the Pagan community, even if it has been denied by most other academics and folklorists since then. Regardless of arguments as to which degree he attained, it gave him a certain credibility that the other occult self-publicist of the day, 'The Great Beast' Aleister Crowley, never obtained, since Crowley left a coven very quickly when he could not agree (according to Gardner) to being 'bossed about by women' and was described by the priestess who expelled him as a 'dirty minded, evilly-disposed, vicious little monster'.

The rituals Gardner allegedly celebrated in the New Forest would have certainly influenced those he wrote and used later, but he was subject to many other influences as well. As a friend of Crowley, he exchanged ideas, and some say Crowley wrote some rituals for him.[4] Others such as Valiente added to them, and it is she whom we must thank for the poetic 'Charge of the Goddess' which is used by many today. There is also a theory that he had contact with members of the Woodcraft Folk movement, and may have been influenced by some of its ideas also. What is most certain is that he also belonged to the OTO (*Ordo Templi Orientis*) for a period, which had its own *grimoire* (an ancient name for a book of spells). Aleister Crowley initiated him into it in 1946 or 1947, depending on which source you believe to be the more accurate, and a letter evidences that he was elevated to the group's seventh degree.[5]

He also became involved with a group of people called the Rosicrucian Crotona Fellowship, running a small Pagan-influenced Rosicrucian Theatre in Christchurch, Hampshire, many of whom were also members of a Co-Masons order, which admitted women. The similarities between some Masonic symbols and ceremonies and those employed by Gardner have been commented upon, but it has always been a matter of conjecture who influenced whom. Of course, it might have been a circular process, with magicians influencing mediaeval Masons, who handed down their Craft, only to feed it back to the modern successors of those earlier Cabbalists, Alchemists and Ceremonial Magicians. For example, the popular Pagan farewell 'Merry meet, merry part and merry may we all meet again' is almost identical to some Masonic wording.

The Path Today

It is ironic that although the Gardnerian Craft was started by some-one seen by many as a renegade from the older order of things, it is nearer to being an orthodoxy than any other European-derived Pagan path. Personally I think Gerald would have thought this sad, as it seems that he was not a man to enjoy people agreeing with him all the time, let alone imitating his every action. Indeed, if one considers the later variations and additions inserted into his *Ye Bok of Ye Art Magical*,[6] he seems to have constantly worked on improving and augmenting his original rituals. Those rituals had first been seen by the public in his novel (a necessary precaution before the repeal of the Witchcraft Act) *High Magic's Aid*, which was published by Michael Houghton in 1949. After the repeal of the Act he was able to write more factually. Three comparative versions of his 'Book of Shadows' are given in *The Witches' Way* (1990) by Janet and Stewart Farrar.

These books reveal the essential nature of the rites he celebrated, and which are still carried on today in either the same or altered forms. They include a ritual feast; dancing in a consecrated circle; a five-fold kiss of the feet, knees, genitalia, breasts, and lips (signifying respect for the whole body, and its purpose in worshipping the Goddess); reverence for male and female deities; and attempts to invoke those deities into their own bodies (termed Drawing Down the Moon), which were most usually naked. Maybe this was influenced by his love of naturism. Being naked is often referred to as being 'skyclad'. Possibly reflecting Gardner's interest in daggers, a ritual sword plus a white-handled knife and an athame (a black-handled knife) were used, along with a cord to bind and to take the measure of new initiates by laying it out around the initiate's silhouette and cutting it. Also used were a chalice cup, bell, wand, incense burner and scourge (which seems to have been a new departure in the history of witchcraft, although of course flagellation was familiar to penitent mediaeval monks).

There are three degrees of initiation, with attainment of the third entitling the recipient to go and form their own coven. There are still original initiates of Gardner's coven alive today, such as Fred Lamond. The authenticity and derivation of one's line of initiation has been very important to many Gardnerians, although this seems less of an issue to others today. If contemplating entering this form of Witchcraft, you might wish to make an independent check on the credentials of someone purporting 'to be of direct line' if it is of personal importance to you.

There have been other important changes made by some of the covens descending from the line of Gardner. Not all practise skyclad nowadays, preferring to be naked beneath a simple robe. The sexual components of male/female initiation (sacred intercourse being termed the Great Rite) have sometimes been changed to a symbolic form. Initiation within Gardnerian Wicca is usually from man to woman or woman to man. Where the couple are already regular sexual partners, the initiation often involves sex between them, while the rest of the coven retires elsewhere. In other cases, the sexual act is symbolised by inserting the athame into the chalice. Gardner did allow for mothers to initiate their daughters and fathers their sons in a non-sexual ceremony, due to the strong family love involved, and probably also as a practical measure.

Nowadays there seems to be a balanced mix of serious ceremonial rituals and more free-form celebration such as wild dancing. The use of trance work seems to have become more popular. In this it is usual for a member to lead a creative visualisation (or 'pathworking') while the coven is in a meditative state, describing a scenario for them to explore within their minds. The rites most often are completed with a ritual feast known as 'cakes and ale'. The ale is more often red wine nowadays, and the cakes are often home-made by a coven member. Sometimes they may be in particular shapes to represent the Moon or a God or Goddess.

Like most religious movements, there have been breakaway groups formed by former adherents, such as Alex Sanders (see Chapter 5) and Ray Buckland (see Chapter 6). Most modern devotees practise both out of doors and in the privacy of their own homes. Gardner actually purchased a 'witch's cottage' from a folk museum and had it erected next to a naturist club to which he belonged in Hertfordshire for convenience.

The attractions of what has become termed Gardnerian Witchcraft are many. It has a structured progression of degrees of teaching and a spiritual path. Even if, as some allege, it was totally invented by Gardner it has still had a successful history of over 50 years. Different covens will teach the various subjects of magical practice (astrology, herbcraft, Craft history, and so on) in a different order, and at a pace suited to the individual, but the expectation is that you will know all you need to know by the stage of taking your final Third Degree. A path that has survived and developed over 50 years has existed for a long time in comparison with other neo-Pagan paths of the twentieth and twenty-first centuries. Additionally, it contains a number of established rites, which have been tried, tested and refined in the light of experience. The patterns of the rituals can be found in the various Books of Shadows that have survived and been published and include initiations and the Drawing Down of the Moon.

Despite so much having been written about it over the years, there is a large element of secrecy within this path, which attracts some and repels others. At initiation one takes on a responsibility not to reveal the identity of other members or to divulge what some of the more secret practices are. The ritual nudity and sexual practices may seem abhorrent to some, but in my own experience I have found Gardnerians to be ethical and moral, with no element of sleaze attaching to them. As with any religion, there may be the occasional 'bad apple', but the majority of High Priests and High Priestesses act as mentors, not dictators, and would not force a member to do anything that they felt uncomfortable with. Their position is not wholly hierarchical, but more 'first among equals', and they are valued for their knowledge and experience without necessarily exercising absolute power. Some covens are more democratic than others in the way that they make decisions.

Of course, the sexual elements mentioned may be the principal attraction to some enquirers, but they are generally disappointed to find that this path is not an excuse for an orgy. One must be clear on one's own standards and principles, and check what is expected within the coven one applies to join. Incidentally, many covens keep people on a waiting list (sometimes for a year and a day) before allowing initiation. Some covens are closed to new members, simply because they are happy with their existing group dynamics and do not wish to change them, which can make it quite hard for a newcomer to find a suitable home. No reputable coven initiates people below the age of 18, and some extend this to 21 or even 25. That wait can be very frustrating to some, and is often seen as a measure of how committed a person is in wanting to join and learn. Some covens set reading or practical exercises to do in the meantime, while others allow limited attendance rights for applicants to a few specific rituals, without being allowed to take any major part in them.

Once initiated into a coven, progress through the degrees will not normally be to any set timetable. When the High Priestess believes you are ready for the next stage of teaching, it will be suggested. It is quite typical for a newcomer to take at least twelve months to progress towards their second degree, and at least another year or two before reaching the third. During that time they will be given increasing responsibilities, and opportunities to deputise for the High Priest or Priestess. Some people choose not to work their way through degrees at all, content to serve as an ordinary first-degree member of a coven.

This shortage of available covens has resulted in some people initiating themselves and setting up covens on Gardnerian principles. There has been much heated debate as to whether people initiated by themselves can claim to be authentic Gardnerians, but one can understand the underlying frustration that causes this. Put against this the classic argument 'Who initiated the first Witch?', and you can see why this issue has resulted in controversy, with accusations of elitism levelled at those who fail to recognise self-initiation as valid. Many Witches will say that the argument fails to take into account the spiritual dimension. It is what happens inside an initiate that counts, regardless of how that process is brought about.

This idea of graduated responsibility is often extended beyond initiation. Although this may cause some frustration, it does mean that initiates can operate in comparative safety to many other paths, and not go into magic too deeply, too quickly. The responsible coven will give only tasks that they think the novice is capable of performing, with a network of support backing that up. Similarly, various members of a coven may be given special responsibilities, such as scrying, herbcraft or cookery, in line with their abilities. (Thus if an important decision is to be taken, the coven astrologer may cast a horoscope, or if a member is sick the herbalist will be called upon.) This allows individuals freedom to specialise and develop in areas that may not interest the rest of the coven, or even be part of the general Gardnerian structure. Many Gardnerians have other interests outside the coven, and may even have a dual allegiance to a Druidic path, for example. Being in a coven formed for the mutual benefit of its members is obviously an advantage if you want support and training within your path. Inevitably, with the strong characters attracted to Paganism, one also has to be aware of the dynamics of any individual group. Some covens also have a social aspect, with parties and outings as part of the general communal activity. Others prefer to keep magical relationships strictly within the coven, and see it as more healthy to have separate outside friends and activities.

While there are set rituals for specific events and seasons, it is evident that most groups have a lot of flexibility in designing their own rituals and developing skills in other areas not necessarily addressed by Gardner. In my opinion (speaking as one with a detached view from outside mainstream witchcraft), his offspring's detractors are generally mistaken in their accusations of rigidity in their thinking, although some may find (at least in theory) the absolute authority invested within the High Priestess as off-putting. This is reflected within the initiation, which asks for 'perfect love and perfect trust' from the candidate, and is a two-way contract of mutual respect.

Things to do

- In the privacy of a room with a full-length mirror, take all your clothes off. Look at your reflection, and analyse what you feel. If you have feelings of shame, inadequacy or poor body image, where do they come from?

- Get a knife (it does not have to be a special ritual one) and practise making the sign of the pentagram in the air with it, watching your progress in the mirror. Hold the knife firmly, pointing it away from the body and make sharply angled, definite movements, describing the shape (as on page 64) in one continuous line. How do you feel about that?

- Think about how you would feel about having a High Priestess as the final arbiter of all coven decisions. She may or may not take the opinions of other members of the coven into consideration.

References

[1] Some say this was a deliberate act by Gardner and Crowley to scare away the 'old guardian spirits of magic' who disliked metal.

[2] Including (it is said) Aleister Crowley, Allan Bennett, Arnold Crowther, Osman Spare, George Pickingill and Cecil Williamson, with whom he worked at the UK's first Witchcraft Museum on the Isle of Man.

[3] He is also said to have been initiated into a coven set up originally by George Pickingill. Although some other Traditional Craft Elders regarded Pickingill as almost heretical, he was acknowledged to be a carrier of the original Tradition. Thus people initiated by him or his covens had to be accepted as authentically part of that same Traditional Craft. Heselton (2000) identifies Dafo as Edith Rose Woodford-Grimes, a teacher of music and elocution, and suggests that she had been taken into the Craft by the Mason family tradition from the south coast of England. I would recommend that you read Heselton & Hutton (1999) if you wish to get a realistic view in detail of Gardner's entry into witchcraft, and subsequent developments.

[4] Valiente says this is unlikely, as she believes they did not meet until Crowley was old and very ill, and that the rituals he started to practise with her in 1953 were close to what he had written in 1949.

[5] The Order derived from Germany just after the turn of the twentieth century. It included ideas connected to Freemasonry, Hinduism and the mystic Eliphas Levi, and appointed Crowley as its English leader in 1912. Gardner seems to have been only active for a year or so before concentrating his energies elsewhere.

[6] This book now resides in Toronto, where it was analysed by the author Aiden Kelly, who states that it was written before the 1953 Gardnerian 'Book of Shadows'. (This dating is crucial in determining who made early contributions to it.) Such books are more commonly called a 'Book of Shadows' nowadays. Each is hand-copied by a magical student from their teachers. Thus it becomes a shadow of all other previous ones, to be added to and subsequently re-copied by subsequent generations. Of course, such a process can be subject to much human error. Doreen Valiente has suggested that the term refers to a Sanskrit manual reviewed in *The Occult Observer* of 1949, which talked about divining a person's destiny from their shadow.

Chapter 5
Alexandrian Wicca

Within Wicca, the mysteries are taught primarily through two sets of ceremonies – a seasonal cycle of festivals in which the focus of the ceremony is on the group as a whole, and initiation rites for an individual or a couple. Initiation rites serve as admission rites but they are also catalysts for psycho-spiritual change. They work on the unconscious mind through symbols that have a profound impact on the psyche.

(Dr Vivianne Crowley, quoted in *Paganism Today*, Harvey and Hardman, 1995)

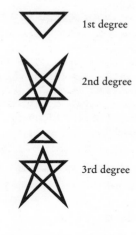

1st degree

2nd degree

3rd degree

Origins

Alex Sanders[1] wished to become a Gardnerian Witch, but could not find a willing initiator. Patricia Crowther, an influential Witch from the North of England, allegedly rejected him but he subsequently was initiated by and worked with Pat Kopanski, who had left Crowther's coven after an argument. He managed to get hold of a Gardnerian 'Book of Shadows', copied it out and thus went on to found his own Alexandrian Wicca, an offshoot of Gardnerian. His partner Maxine Sanders, who separated from him in the 1970s, aided him in all of this. He also developed its rites, and came up with some ideas of his own, including self-initiation, a principle that has been the subject of much controversy since. At one stage he claimed to have been initiated by his grandmother in her kitchen, but later refuted it although it is known he came from a family of Welsh Spiritualist mediums. (Gardner too had been interested in Spiritualism when younger.) Maybe his initial problems in seeking initiation pushed him into trying to side-step it in one way or another, but in the end he was responsible for an important shift in attitude towards Witchcraft.

For those who believe a continuous line of traditional initiation back to a Traditional or Hereditary source is important, Alexandrian provenance may prove an insurmountable problem. Having said that, it is a line of over 40 years long in itself, and many more traditionalist views on initiation have faded in the last decade, in the light of a too large a number of people wanting initiation into a small number of covens unable to accommodate them all.

King of the Witches

Even without the issue of self-initiation, Alex Sanders was a controversial character, who courted media publicity and accepted being dubbed the 'King of the Witches'. This clearly annoyed many other Witches, who accepted and recognised no such leader, and therefore denounced him. Coincidentally, there is a practice in some other forms of Witchcraft of having a King and Queen Witch, but not in the usual sense of the words, and it is doubtful whether Sanders was referring to that process.

If a coven produces members who attain third degree, and who go off with the blessing of their mother coven to set up covens of their own, the High Priest and Priestess of the original coven are said to be King and Queen if they parent three other covens. This is not a right of rule, but of Elder consultative status. Certainly, Alex and Maxine were the progenitors of many more than three covens, so under those circumstances could rightly claim the titles, though not in a way that would give them a hierarchical status over every other

Witch. Among their initiates were the well-respected Janet and Stewart Farrar. Stewart had originally met Sanders as a reporter, and wrote a book about him called *What Witches Do* (1971).

Differences

Just as Gardner continued to amend and refine his rituals, so did Sanders. Inevitably this produced some differing practices over the years, although they originate from the same sources and are very similar. In later life Sanders proposed ways in which homosexuals could be accommodated within Wicca, who had been avoided until then by most practitioners. The Farrars (1990) mention how in Alexandrian Witchcraft the initiate is introduced slightly differently into the circle, and the fact that Alexandrians give the measure cord back to initiates, while Gardnerians retain it at least for a time.

There used to be a certain uneasiness between the two traditions, but in my own experience they seem to get on fairly well together nowadays, appreciating that they have more in common than separating them. One will sometimes hear jokes poking fun at each tradition's stereotypical attribute, but this tends to be good-natured ribbing between friends rather than hostility.

Things to do

- Consider your attitudes towards homosexuals and lesbians. Where do your views originate from, and have they changed over a period of time? Would you feel comfortable working magically with them?

- Pagans sometimes make fun of other sorts of Pagans. How do you feel about that? What if it was a non-Pagan making a joke about your beliefs and customs – would the same rules apply?

References

[1] Originally Orrell Alexander Carter (1926–88).

Chapter 6
Later Offshoots, Including Seax and Progressive Witchcraft

To find a form that accommodates the mess, that is the task of the artist now. (Samuel Becket in *Proust*)

Air   Fire   Water   Earth

Seax Wicca

In such an individualistic area of spirituality, it is inevitable that adherents of one path become creators of new ones. Raymond Buckland, a Gardnerian, developed his thinking about Saxon mythology and written records to produce a new form around 1973–4, which he called Seax Wicca. It was publicised via his book *The Tree: the Complete book of Saxon Witchcraft* (1974) and at the time of publishing was thought controversial for its inclusion of a self-initiation rite. Since then attitudes have changed, and even those of a more traditional Craft inclination have accepted this as an inevitable result of the growth of Wicca when there are insufficient existing covens to take on new initiates.

Unlike some of the founders of several other paths, Buckland was very honest in his creation of Seax Wicca, not claiming ancient sources or mystical channelling. He quite openly states that Seax Wicca is of his own making (with help from his partner Tara). Seax

Wicca was influenced by Gardnerian Witchcraft and other paths, but it has been developed into an individual, recognisable form practised in many countries. Although the beliefs and practices are explained in that single book, there is an expectation that followers will be wider read and aware of other forms of Witchcraft, rather than reliant on one person's teachings. It is interesting to note that although Buckland kept his own Gardnerian oath of secrecy, he deliberately created a system with completely open, published rites and no secrecy.

The path is based on what Buckland thought were basic Saxon Pagan beliefs. These are sometimes quite hard to identify since the Saxons had a long time to develop different forms of Paganism, and were influenced by a variety of other forms from outside their own culture, such as those of the Norse and Celtic peoples. The path differs from Asatru (see Chapter 9), since it deliberately applies the Saxon mythology as a basis for Witchcraft, whereas most Asatru followers do not class themselves as Witches. It also has a rune script, which is different from the historical ones. (Runes are a magical alphabet, used for divination, spells and ritual, as well as reading and writing.)

Buckland believed that Seax Wicca should continue to develop and be augmented, just as the Saxons' beliefs had evolved. He therefore encouraged Seax Wiccans to create their own new rituals and incorporate any useful material from elsewhere. Consequently there is no such thing as a typical Seax Wiccan ritual or practitioner.

> The encouragement to add to the tradition can lead to eclecticism run rampant. Researching the roots of Paganism and Witchcraft can lead to a mixing of cultures that can be quite confusing to a new practitioner of Seax Wicca. However, many good covens try to break out what has been added to the tradition from Buckland's teachings and truly try not confuse cultures and practices. (Daven, Witchvox website)

One key difference, however, is that the main rituals (most of which are very short and simple) are linked to the solar cycle, unlike most other forms of Wicca, which follow the lunar phases. Having said that, Seax are free to conduct rites at the full Moon (or other phases) as well. God and Goddess are regarded as equals, as are the priest and priestess. However, the Lord is said to be the dominant force in winter (Samhain to Beltane) and the Lady for the summer half of the year.

Another major difference is that covens are run democratically, electing a priest and priestess for a year. There are no formal initiations or degrees, other than the newcomer's original self-declaration on joining of the coven. Also, the athame ritual metal knife is used for cutting and everyday jobs, unlike most other traditions that keep it exclusively for directing magical energy. The theory behind this is that using it practically in everyday situations will imprint your personality and feelings upon it. Consequently, Seax Wicca has no place for the white-handled *boline* knife, used for cutting herbs and so on in many other Wiccan traditions. In fact, few tools are used; one addition is the spear, held by the Thegn (pronounced thain). The Thegn calls the members to the ritual, draws the circle and is charge of facilitating it. Other officers are the Scribe (a type of secretary/treasurer) and the Priest and Priestess.

Progressive Witchcraft

Progressive Wicca is less of an offshoot, and more of a change of emphasis for some existing Gardnerian and Alexandrian and other Witches, who wanted more freedom to experiment with new practices. Some individuals will have dual membership of a Progressive coven and a Gardnerian or Alexandrian one. Many Progressives believe it is important to have a solid grounding in one of the older traditions before experimenting with its newer form, and it differs from Eclectic Witchcraft in that it prefers (but does not insist) practitioners to have been initiated into a tradition.

> We do not see our 'trainees' as empty vessels, waiting to be filled up, but as individuals with a wealth of experience and ideas which they can contribute to the craft. (Rainbird, 1993)

Although they use a degree system, covens are run democratically, and the High Priest and Priestess roles alternate around suitable members. There are a few specifically male or female Progressive Wicca groups, and there has been experimentation into Drawing Down the Goddess into males, and the God into females. Not a lot has been written about this particular strand of Witchcraft, maybe because it is less a tradition and more a way of thinking about traditions. One book has been published principally for solo Witches interested in this area, called *Magick Without Peers* (Rainbird and Rankine, 1995).

Georgian Wicca

There are many more individual Wiccan traditions forming, sub-dividing, dissolving and re-forming. Some are very similar, while others reflect the individual personalities of their originators. In most religious paths this would be frowned upon, but the Pagan scene in general celebrates its diversity and individuality, recognising the right of everyone to be their own priest or priestess, and to have a direct and very personal relationship with their deities. One such path is Georgian Wicca, founded by the late George 'Pat' Patterson in America in the 1970s. His advice was to take what felt the best and most appropriate practices from Gardnerian, Alexandrian and other paths, adding and discarding elements to one's personal taste. Because of this, no two Georgians are likely to practise in the same way, but will both have the same guiding principles. Inevitably, some experimental and breakaway groups do not survive very long, or spread very far, but Seax, Progressive and Georgian Wicca have all survived and spread over a period of several years.

Things to do

- If you are thinking of becoming a Pagan, try writing an oath of dedication, stating the ways you want to follow and the code of ethics you wish to obey. Prepare yourself by bathing, or even fasting, and conduct the oath-taking in whatever way seems appropriate to you. You can do this on your own or invite sympathetic friends as witnesses. Remember though, the ultimate witnesses are yourself and the Gods and Goddesses, whom you should address directly, asking their help and understanding. Do not worry if the ritual is imperfect in its execution. It is the intention of your heart that is important.

Chapter 7
Hedgewitch Traditions

What Chekhov saw in our failure to communicate was something positive and precious: the private silence in which we live, and which enables us to endure our own solitude. We live, as his characters do, beyond any tale we happen to enact. (VS Pritchett)

What is a Hedgewitch?

Although we often think of Witches working together in a coven, historically it is far more likely that most worked alone, with only occasional contact with others of their kind. The majority of Witch trials of the sixteenth and seventeenth centuries were directed towards individuals, despite witch hunters such as Matthew Hopkins attempting to force confessions out of the accused that would implicate confederates, which would inevitably have increased his income. While it could be argued that his unfortunate victims were being brave and shielding their comrades, most historical sources (such as those on view at the Museum of Witchcraft in Boscastle, Cornwall) suggest that the solitary Witch would have been most common. This idea has found new currency within modern Paganism, with the coining of the term (and the book title) *Hedgewitch* by the author Rae Beth (1992) and the writings and lectures of Marion Green, including *A Witch Alone* (1991) and *Elements of Natural Magic* (1997).

By their very nature, solitary Witches tend to work in simpler, less ritualistic ways than those in covens, although this is a generalisation, which has many honourable exceptions. They will tend to be more concerned with herbalism than Hermeticism,[1] and despite having little contact with other Witches, very often have proportionally more contact with their local communities, for whom they perform healing and other services. I have a theory that such solo Witches are more accessible to a local village culture than a secretive coven, and will be judged on results and reputation, even if their beliefs seem eccentric. There is one Witch of my acquaintance, Cassandra Latham of Cornwall, who openly derives her main living this way, and is registered as such with the tax authorities just like any other self-employed businesswoman. Hedgewitches may align themselves with any one of a number of mythologies and cultures, from Celtic and Saxon through to Egyptian and Finnish-Sami, or be completely eclectic.

I think that there are two main reasons why people seek to become Hedgewitches. Firstly, if they are of a very independent nature, do not enjoy group rituals and do not wish to compromise their ideals and methods by working within a group, then the tradition accommodates that. Secondly, some are forced into it by not having access to a group, or not wishing to expose their beliefs to others. Because of their independent nature they may also be completely unaware of or not interested in the existence of other Pagans in their area. Of course, some Hedgewitches prefer to work mainly that way, but also enjoy occasional contact with other Pagans at moots, conferences and joint rituals. They may also derive support and networking through magazines and the Hedgewitches' Association (even if an association for those who prefer to be independent does on the face of it seem contradictory).

Although practising as a solo Witch brings much more freedom of expression, it often also has the drawback of not having a local network of support and advice. The Hedgewitch has to be very single-minded and dedicated to self-development through private study for the most part. There is, however, for the Hedgewitch the extra self-satisfaction of having done things for oneself, rather than relying on others.

Things to do

- Make a list of the types of activities you would like to incorporate into your personal religious methodology, such as meditation, Tarot, ritual, Egyptian deities, and so on. Also make a list of things you would not like to be involved in. Can you see any pattern, or spiritual path that they would point you to? Do not worry if they do not. Keep the list and ask the same question after you have read the whole book.

References

[1] Hermeticism is Ancient Egyptian magic, connected with the God Thoth.

Chapter 8
Druidry

Nuinn[1] now entered, distinguished as the Chief by a golden emblem of the Three Bars of Light placed on his head-dress – at the point of the brow chakra, the Third Eye. 'Let us begin by giving peace to the quarters, for without peace can no work be. Peace to the North. Peace to the South. Peace to the West. Peace to the East. May there be peace throughout the world.' (Phillip Carr-Gomm, quoted in Jones and Matthews, 1990)

What is Druidry?

Druidry is unusual within the Pagan world, in that it is equally biased towards a triad of Solar, Lunar and Earth veneration. Coupled with this is the fact that, unlike Witches, Druids are publicly accepted as a somewhat archaic, slightly eccentric part of Britain's traditional heritage, in the same way as morris dancers are. Their public gatherings of Bards (known as Gorseddau), some in flowing white or other coloured robes, are held in full view at Stonehenge and Primrose Hill, London, although far more private celebrations are held in sacred woodland groves and other outdoor sites of natural beauty.

There are as many different interpretations as to what Druidry is as there are individual Druids. Certainly it is a spiritual discipline, but it is not exclusively Pagan. Its ranks also include Christians, Buddhists and other religious groups, although they would mostly agree that there is a central core of belief which allows them to interpret the idea of *Awen*, an all-pervading life force, in their own separate ways, and to recognise that all religions reflect one basic central set of truths. Emma Restall Orr of the British Druid Order said the following to me:

> Druidry is exquisitely simple. Indeed it is almost painfully so, for as a spiritual quest, like craving for a holy grail, we stumble down paths bramble-tangled with hopes and justifications, before realising it is so. Druidry is the sacred relationship between the people and these islands. It's a religion wrapped in history, heritage, language, the beauty of these lands, the seas that shape them, the skies above, abundant greens, soft mists, summer storms, wild roses, the natural tides of living and dying.

Druidry's openness and lack of secrecy is certainly an attraction to many, who appreciate its tolerance, peaceful emphasis and established existence. Its direct connection to the Celtic world is especially relevant to many, and the breadth and diversity of groupings makes it possible to find a close match for any particular viewpoint. There are also some Druidic orders that are non-religious, stemming from the eighteenth-century revival and Welsh nationalism. They are mainly of Welsh extraction, and concentrate on promoting Eisteddfod arts festivals and preserving the Welsh language and poetic and musical forms. There are even some Druidic-named mutual friendly insurance groups. Druid orders are found in the Celtic areas, Brittany, Wales, Scotland, Ireland and Cornwall, although some would insist that it is more about 'Britain' than any specific Celtic area, and that there are more Druids in the UK and USA outside of these areas than within them.

> The search for 'authentic' Druidry is like shooting arrows at the moon: both activities are essentially futile, but are great fun for their own sake. If we take it that British Druidry existed in its purest form before the arrival of the Romans in 43 BCE, then we have to face the sad fact that the Druids of that time did not leave us a single written account of any of their myths or ceremonies. We are left with the fragmentary, biased and usually second- or third-hand accounts of Celtic religion given by Greek and Roman writers, and with what archaeologists can recover from physical remains. (Phillip Shallcrass of OBOD, quoted in Harvey and Hardman, 1996)

There are Roman descriptions of Druids as the specially-protected priests and priestesses, judges, seers and advisors of the Britons that they were trying to conquer. They saw them as a threat, since they were a unifying force within the collection of warring tribes, and the Romans killed a great many of them on Mona's Isle (Ynys Mon), which is present-day Anglesey in North Wales. They also (along with subsequent waves of invaders such as the Saxons and the Normans) destroyed the sacred tree groves in which the Druids celebrated their religion. Inevitably, some Druids survived as individual travelling holy men and women, and when Christianity took root it is said that some males became priests of the new religion. As an educated elite, they had reading, writing and mathematical skills, and held honoured positions at royal courts for their accumulated wisdom and wise counsel.

> Druidry is based upon the love of the natural world, and offers a powerful way of working with and understanding the Self and Nature – speaking to that level of our soul and of our being which is in tune with the elements and the stars, the sun and the stones. Through the work of the Druids we are able to unite our natural, earthy selves with our spiritual selves while working, in however small a way, for the safeguarding of our planet. (Leaflet of the Order of Bards, Ovates and Druids)

You will notice from the name of that Order that Druidry is generally divided into three grades. Traditionally the training period for each grade was seven years, although attitudes to this have changed, partly due to different training methods and a change in emphasis as to what is relevant to modern culture. Some people now devote their whole life to a single discipline, while others either accelerate the pace or try to combine all three. The stages are not exclusive, as each will also call upon the skills and techniques of the others.

Bards are most concerned with learning and performing the stories, songs and poetry of their culture, which formed the framework for later personal development. This was done historically by memorising much material, rather than writing notes. The Druids did develop a form of writing known as ogham script, a series of lines carved on two adjacent edges of a piece of wood or stone, which is symbolic of varieties of tree and other natural elements. They would also be expected to compose new songs and poems to commemorate memorable deeds, and finding a personal form of artistic expression is still very much a part of this role.

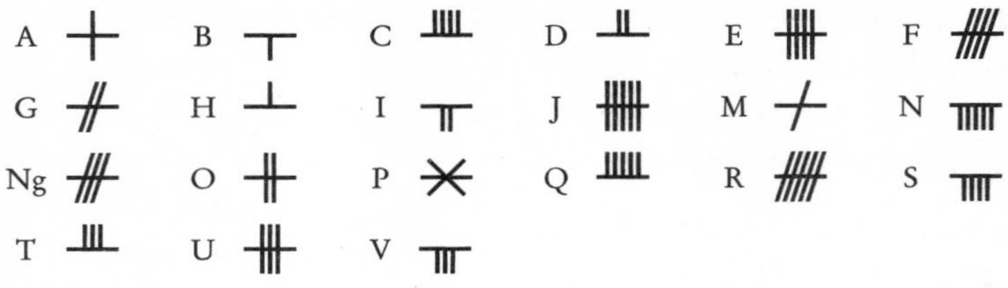
A
B
C
D
E
F
G
H
I
J
M
N
Ng
O
P
Q
R
S
T
U
V

Druidic Ogham alphabet – the central line represents the angled corner of the stone

Ovates study medicine, herbs, botany, astronomy and astrology, which has resulted in their being regarded as the seers of their culture. They tend to work in more shamanic ways than those of the Bardic grouping.

Druids combine the elements of the other grades together, and become teachers, priests and advisors, combining the work of the Bards' physical world with that of the Ovates' other-worldly experiences. One elderly Druid of my acquaintance said, 'The worst bit of reaching this stage was to understand how little one really knew.'

The Mythology

Once again, it is difficult to generalise, but most Druids draw upon the Celtic mythology and/or Arthurian legend. Some of this is very complex, with hidden layers of symbolism and some very confusingly similar characters' names of difficult pronunciation, especially if you are not a native speaker of Welsh, Irish, Cornish or Breton. Some of the stories come from the Welsh *Mabinogion* or the Irish *Book of Tain*. The Arthurian legends referred to are frequently those from Brittany, rather than the more familiar British versions.

Festivals

It should be noted that some Druids prefer to observe the old pre-1752 calendar, which alters the fire festival dates by 11 days. As well as the usual Celtic fire festivals (Samhain, Imbolc, Beltane and Lughnasagh), Druids celebrate the following Solar festivals:

Winter Solstice (*Alban Arthuan* – Light of Arthur) approximately 21 December.

Spring Equinox (*Alban Eilur* – Light of the Earth) approximately 21 March.

Summer Solstice (*Alban Heruin* – Light of the Shore) approximately 21 June.

Autumn Equinox (*Alban Elued* – Light of the Water) approximately 21 September.

The Awen

Central to all modern Druidic belief is the principle labelled as *Awen*. It means 'flowing spirit', an all-pervading creative life force, and is applied to every Druidic activity from being aware of the properties of trees through to making poetry. It is also used as a repetitive mantra or chant in the form 'Ah-oo-en'.

It is very difficult to define what Druids believe, since they are very diverse, but I think the following quotation would find favour with many, though not all:

> Therefore Druids hold the understanding of ultimately the one unknowable source of all being, that in fact we have no one name for, though it has been called the great spirit, Ceugant, the source. This source flows through everything there is, in all worlds at all times. It is that which is beyond our human understanding but in no way separate from us for we are 'of it'. It is the divine power of love and life that even death is part of. Death is change, it gives birth to new life. (Worthington, 1999)

In the eighteenth and nineteenth centuries, a passion for the ideals of the 'noble savage' and arcane wisdom resulted in a revived interest and flowering of Druidry. New orders, which included notable enthusiasts such as William Blake, were created, in a line that extends until today. One individual who had an enormous influence on the nineteenth- and twentieth-century revival of Druidry was Iolo Morganwg.[2] Like many other individuals mentioned in this book, he has his detractors, and the movement has moved on from some of the issues relevant just to his era, but it is doubtful whether we would have seen such a flowering of modern Druidism without his vision, enthusiasm and energy.

There are many Druid orders in existence today. Some are large and well organised, whilst others comprise just a handful of members. Some offer practical training, and many orders belong to the Council of British Druid Orders (COBDO), which liaises on issues of common interest. Each order has a unique flavour, with some claiming a greater antiquity and lineage. It is worth enquiring widely to find the one that reflects your own attitudes and aspirations. Their rituals are often very beautiful, incorporating much poetry and music, and their skill at providing meaningful ritual for general crowds of interested onlookers is not to be under-estimated.

Druids have an image of calm, measured responses, but I was much taken with the eco-warrior stance taken by King Arthur Pendragon, a controversial and provocative figure in Druid circles who leads the Loyal Arthurian Warband:

> 'Who's more the Druid, the protestor up in the tree, or the guy on the ground wearing the white frock?' Although both are arguable, Arthur's answer was: 'The guy up the tree in the white frock, the Loyal Arthurian Warband!' (David Smith, 2000)

Things to do

- Druids are unusual among Pagans in that they are equally concerned with the Sun, Earth and Moon. Why not get up early one morning, and go to a quiet natural place such as the hills or seashore, and watch the sunrise? Be aware of the landscape you are in. The Earth on which you stand is as important as the Sun and Moon to Druids and other Pagans.

- Either later that day, or another time, give yourself time and space to enjoy a sunset.

References

[1] Real name Phillip Ross Nichols, Chief of the Order of Bards, Ovates and Druids. Carr-Gomm succeeded him.

[2] Real name Edward Williams, who lived in the seventeenth century. He produced a book called *Barddas*, which is the subject of some dispute. Some argue that it contains a forgery of older documents, alongside some of his own personal theories. Whatever the case, this book has sustained the revival with some ideas that are

worthwhile, regardless of their origin. One of the principal ideas is of three circles of experience, or travel through life. *Annwn*, the cauldron of birth and rebirth, is at the centre, with three rings spreading from it. *Abred* is the physical realm, *Gwynvid* of the enlightened spirits and *Ceugant* the sphere of ultimate Creator. It has been argued that the concentric circles are reversed, i.e. *Annwn* on the outside, progressing to *Ceugant* at the core.

Chapter 9
Asatru and the Northern Tradition

Flags, Flax, Fodder and Frigg! (Traditional Saxon-derived blessing, meaning may you have a hearth, clothes, food and sex.)

What is the Northern Tradition?

Someone once called the Northern Tradition 'Paganism with attitude' and it's true that this uniquely distinct form of Paganism is very direct in its approach, and is not for the faint-hearted. It draws upon the mythology and folk beliefs of the Scandinavian, Teutonic and Saxon races; both in their homelands and in the places they later settled, including Great Britain, the Orkneys, Iceland, Greenland and America. Today it very much appeals to Pagans who are independent-minded and who are prepared to work at their own straightforward path rather than be spoon-fed an established system.

The Northern Tradition goes under a variety of names. Asatru means being true to the Asa, a collective name for the Gods and Goddesses. (It used to be thought it referred only to the Aesir family of Gods, but modern thinking invests the Asa term with a more generally inclusive feel, taking in the Vanir deities as well.) Because it is derived from the Teutonic tribes of Northern Europe, it has also become known as the Northern Tradition or the Norse or Viking Tradition. A few of its celebrants prefer to be referred to as Heathens (similar in meaning to the Latin 'Pagan', and derived from the Germanic for 'living on the heath', meaning that practitioners follow the old rural practices). Another term is Odinism, after the chief God. This term is somewhat misleading since most Odinists acknowledge a number of deities, not just Odin. Although they go under many different names, most members of the Northern Tradition have similar beliefs and get on very well with each other.

Historical Background

The Vikings are often referred to as a race, but the word in fact means to 'go a-pirating',[1] and the term could cover people of Danish, Norwegian, Jutish, Angle, Frisian or Saxon stock. Contrary to the Victorian-generated popular belief, they did not wear horned helmets to war (which would have been impractical) and, although they did do a lot of bloodthirsty raiding, were no worse than any other tribal group of the time. Their bad press mainly stems from the people who wrote the historical records – the monks whose wealthy monasteries they looted.

The Vikings explored in their innovative dragon ships, trading and settling over a wide area, creating towns in Russia (hauling their boats over mountain passes), Great Britain (such as York, or 'Jorvik' as it was then known) and Ireland (such as Dublin). From settling in the Orkneys, Iceland and Greenland, they eventually sent an expedition to America, headed by Leif Eriksson, where they set up a short-lived settlement predating Columbus by several hundred years. This was thought a myth for many years until firm evidence was found at L'Anse-aux-Meadows, Newfoundland. They called America 'Vinland', after the vines they found there.

The Vikings created the basis of our modern legal system, with a set of fixed penalties for damages. They created working democracies, loved playing board games, wearing amber and other beautiful jewellery, and more of them farmed and traded than raided. One was not thought to be a proper leader if unable to compose poetry and argue points of law as well as being a warrior. Because they intermarried with local people, and respected the Gods of their new homelands, they were often quickly converted to Christianity.

Asatru Today

The Northern Tradition has increased in size over the last few years, and now attracts far more women than it used to. Originally it suffered from an image of the aggressive macho Viking warrior, but it has a much broader appeal and range of role models than that. Of course, this machismo can also be an attraction to some women who want to act in a warrior fashion.

At one time, many of this path kept themselves aloof, not wishing their rites to be over-influenced by other practices such as Wicca. However, now that information is more readily available and specific rituals have been published, what was once a misunderstood specialisation has grown to take its place within and be accepted by the Pagan mainstream. For example, I am a well-known Odinist, and was elected the President of the Pagan Federation in 1997, whereas most, if not all, of my predecessors had been Wiccan. I do not think that would have been considered likely a few years previously. However, I have to admit that a fair number of my comrades do still remain slightly aloof from mainstream Paganism, and are far less likely to adopt eclectic practices from other traditions, not through elitism but because they feel their own system is complete. There is also a misplaced reluctance by some other Pagans to engage with them due to misunderstood ideas about their beliefs.

Beliefs and Ritual

The main deities include (dual Norse/Saxon names given where appropriate) Odin/Woden, Thor/Thunor, Tyr/Tiw, Frigga, Balder, Frey and Freyja.[2] However, the Norse pantheon includes over 100 deities in total, subdivided into the Aesir and the Vanir. (There are also *wights* or *landvaettir*, who are revered as spirits of the landscape.)[3] The Vanir tend to be the older entities, personifying natural elements such as waterfalls, woods and rocks. The Aesir, who are said to have overcome them, tend to represent aspects of civilisation and agriculture, but can have natural attributes as well, such as Thor's thunder. The mythology is very complex and beautiful. The stories centre around the world tree Yggdrassil (thought by some to be an ash, but by others including myself to be a yew), containing nine worlds that are often under attack from the Thurz giants, personification of violent natural forces. I have mapped out its complicated geography in my book *Norse Tradition* (1998).

Much of our knowledge of the mythology comes from two Icelandic texts, the Prose Edda and the Poetic Edda, plus a number of sagas.[4] It is easy to forget that the mythology we have today is the incomplete remnants of a set of stories evolving over many different countries for about 700 years (300–1000 CE).[5] A villager in fourth-century Sweden would not necessarily be familiar with the range of stories known by an eleventh-century Icelander, or even worship familiar Gods with the same names. There are inevitably inconsistencies and contradictions, and further confusion has been added with the inaccuracies in such works as Wagner's Ring Cycle. This is compounded by the use of eke-names (or nicknames) for the deities. You can never be sure when reading a name in a literary source whether it is a deity new to you, or one of the many alternatives appended to a well-known God. One particular feature that sets the tradition apart is giving the Moon a male characteristic, and the Sun a feminine polarity, on the basis of a man being cold and hard, and a woman warm and embracing. (The Celts reverse this with the Moon being dark and mysterious like a woman and the Sun hot and aggressive like a man. Of course both ideas are stereotypes.)

There is also a belief in a predetermined fate called *orlog* or *Wyrd* for each person, decided upon by the Norns (the equivalent of the Greek Fates), who spin, weave and cut the thread of the individual's existence. The Norns are called Skuld, Urd and Verdandi, which translate as Being, Fate and Necessity respectively (not Past, Present and Future as it is sometimes erroneously given). Sometimes this idea is symbolised by a spider's web; if you touch one fibre, reverberations are felt and affect the rest of the interconnected structure. This concept is also often applied to the tribal or family group, in having a collective 'luck' that can be influenced for good or ill down several generations by the act of one individual member. Hence honouring your ancestors is an important activity, especially when considers that within the earliest Norse beliefs a person's reputation was all that ensured their immortality, since there was no concept of heaven and hell. Later beliefs featured a heaven called Asgard where good warriors were selected by the Valkyries to continue feasting and fighting, Freya's Sessrunner hall for families and Hel as a rather duller sort of afterlife. Although Hel was demonised in late myths, the earlier one of Balder's death depicted it as being more pleasant and featuring eating and drinking.

Central to the beliefs is the idea of *Troth* – a voluntary obligation to be loyal and do the right thing by one's Gods, family and friends, to keep oaths and to act in an honourable way, taking responsibility for one's actions. There is a form of moral code and advice on giving and receiving hospitality in a document called the *Hávamal* (Sayings of the High One), but example is also taken from the other sagas and books available. Many Odinists live by what are termed the Nine Noble Virtues, which vary slightly according to source, but can be summarised as Courage, Fidelity, Industriousness, Truth, Discipline, Self-reliance, Honour, Hospitality and Perseverance.

Oath-taking is still an important part of Norse ritual. Oaths are taken upon a special arm ring, which is sometimes bathed in blood from the meat to be eaten in the ritual feast. The name for a ritual is *blot* (rhymes with boat), which indicates the use of blood being liberally sprinkled around in ancient rituals. Other features of modern ritual (which is conducted in an open air rectangular sacred space called a *ve*)[6] are the drinking of horns of mead and a *sumbul*, a form or ritual boasting and oath-taking. A *mjollnir* (Thor's hammer) is used to hallow and purify the celebrants and their ritual tools. Chants and dance are also used, as are especially composed poems. A rite is likely to start and finish with a loud '*Waes Hael!*', a greeting which translates as 'be hale and healthy!'. This is the meaning behind the wassail cup, and the wishing luck by singing and making a noise in English midwinter folk customs.

Followers may celebrate alone or together in hearths, sometimes also called *garths*, *kindreds* or *godhords*. Some of these local groups are independent, while others are associated with larger organisations. Male and female are ranked equal (ancient Norse women could divorce, own land and vote at the *Thing* or council assembly) and either sex may lead a hearth, although there is little hierarchy or degree system beyond this. The priest and priestess are called *gothi* and *gytha* respectively, and there is also a female shamanic seeress role known as a *volva*. A male shaman or runemaster is sometimes referred to as a *vitki*.

There are two distinct forms of magic, *seidr* and *galdr*, but only a small proportion of Odinists practise magic. Galdr is a more ceremonial ritual form of magic, mostly practised by the priest or priestess, whilst the more shamanic, intuitive seidr (literally, 'seething') is the main province of the volva and vitki. However, there is an overlap, and each will borrow the other's techniques while concentrating on their own.

Some American authors have published numerous forms of ritual and runic practice, which they have personally developed, including the influential Edred Thorsson (1984, 1987, 1988, 1992) and Ed Fitch (1990). More recently Kvendulf Gundarsson (1990, 1993) has produced some interesting views on Teutonic magic and religion, which are well worth investigating if you are looking for ideas that reflect more recent research.

The Runes

The mystical and magical runes are also central to the Northern Tradition's mysteries. These are chanted, inscribed as spells and copied in bodily posture, as well as being used for divination. Sometimes three or more are combined together to make a bindrune spell. The runes are a set of magical alphabets, varying in size and nature, which can be used to read and write with. Each alphabet is known as a *futhark* (from the sound of the first six characters) and is divided into *aetts*, or families of eight. The most popular Norse Elder Futhark has 24 runes, while the Anglo-Saxon has 16 and the Northumbrian 32, with extra variations coming in over the approximately 700-year period of their main use.

There are dozens of books with completely different interpretations of the meanings of the runes. While those interpretations may be correct for the individual authors, based on their own meditations, I would always suggest going back to the old rune poems, and developing your own ideas from the simple, basic interpretations

Freyjas Aett	ᚠ	ᚢ	ᚦ	ᚨ	ᚱ	ᚲ	ᚷ	ᚹ
	f	u	th	a	r	k	g	w
Hagels Aett	ᚺ	ᚾ	ᛁ	ᛃ	ᛇ	ᛈ	ᛉ	ᛊ
	h	n	i	j	eo	p	y	s
Tyrs Aett	ᛏ	ᛒ	ᛖ	ᛗ	ᛚ	ᛜ	ᛞ	
	t	b	e	m	l	o	d	

The Elder Futhark of Runes

found there. Runes are a powerful tool, and should be treated as potentially dangerous; they are not merely to be played with.

Norse Cults

A group of elements of Norse belief and culture which have attracted surprisingly little interest or published research, are the berserker warrior cults. Berserker means 'bear-shirted', suggesting that their totemic animal was a bear, which they either physically or symbolically killed, taking on its skin and spirit. There are several accounts of berserkers going into a much feared battle frenzy, when they fought with the strength of several men, with no apparent fear of injury to themselves. Their very presence sometimes resulted in an opposing force backing down as they intimidated them by biting their shields, casting off clothes and metaphorically, if not physically, foaming at the mouth. In the early tales they are much valued as warriors, but in later sagas (possibly told from a Christian perspective) they degenerate into bullyboy robbers, to be got rid of by some hero or other. There is also at least one saga where a berserker projects himself psychically by means of a *fylga* (sending out a controlled spiritual entity) bear into a battle.[7] The Saxon hero Hereward the Wake (who fought the Normans, themselves an offshoot of the Norse peoples) appears in some stories to have been a berserker as well, so it may also have been an aspect of Anglo-Saxon culture.

Similar in nature, but not so much in evidence, were the *Ulfhednar* wolf cult, as well as a group with but a single reference, the *Chati*, a cat cult. Better known in both Norse and Saxon society was the dedication of *Svinfylking* warriors to a totem of Frey, the boar, and a few helmets with a boar crest have been excavated. It is thought that followers often fought in a V-formation, with two members at its angle (or snout).

Organisations

There are several organisations catering for Odinists around the world, with no single one being particularly dominant. I do have to add a note of warning here, in that in a minority of exceptional cases, far right or neo-Nazi groups have tried to recruit via the Odinist community. This is a throwback to the Nazis of World War Two usurping runes and Norse mythology in a vain effort to justify their Aryan super-race theories. The general Odinist community shuns this misuse of their religion in the same way that other religions have shunned perversions of their particular beliefs. Many do believe in general that one's spiritual path should be generated from one's racial roots. However, this is not the same as saying that other races are inferior, but rather that they are different and have equally valid paths of their own appropriate to the landscape and tribes within which they were founded. This is the difference between a patriot and a racist: a patriot says 'My country is great,' but a racist says 'My country is greatest.'

In the UK Odinshof and the Ring of Troth are two well-respected national Odinist organisations. Odinshof has successfully raised funds to buy and preserve woodland for heathen use, and offers a gothi training course run by myself (Jennings, 1998 and 2000).[8] Ring of Troth concentrates more on training in the seidr magic under the dynamic leadership of notable Odinist author Freya Aswynn (2000). The UK-based Ring of Troth is the European arm of an American-based organisation of the same name. There is also a branch of a Swedish family tradition group based in the UK called Hammarans Ordens Sallskap, which is much concerned with practical environmental issues.

In the USA itself, there are also a couple of Anglo-Saxon based heathen organisations, Theod and Anglo-Saxon Eldright, as well as the Asatru Free Assembly and lots of locally-based general Odinist kindreds. Some of these are very large and put on ambitious three-day events. Asatru is a force to be reckoned within both the UK and the American Pagan community and elsewhere nowadays.

Things to do

- Try to find out if the Vikings invaded or immigrated into your geographic area. Clues are sometimes given by place names, such as town names ending in *-by*, *-thwaite* and *-fell*, and street names ending in *-gate* or *-score/skaw*, *-beck*, *-kirk* and *-gill*. Saxon place names often end in *-ham* (homestead), *-ing* (people of) and *-ton* (farm). Sometimes you can find a name with elements of both, such as Kirton in Suffolk, made from Norse *kirk* (church) and Saxon *ton* (farm.) You can also look for place names with 'harrow' (*hearg*) in them or Grim, such as Grimsdyke or Grimes Graves, which is an eke-name for Woden in his hooded form.

- Have you tried mead? It is a special alcoholic beverage produced from honey. Why not try some to drink?

- If you have access to a suitable museum, such as the Jorvik Centre in York, England, or Osberg in Sweden, why not go and look at some Viking artefacts? Their jewellery, ships and carvings are very beautiful.

References

[1] Many of the Scandinavian raiders and traders left from the port of Vik (or Vikbolandet) in Sweden. *Vik* means a creek or inlet, which is the way they gained access to the settlements they travelled to, and *ing* means 'man' or 'the people of', so the term *Viking* was an appropriate one. Incidentally, most people in Britain referred to them as Danes, regardless of whether they came from Norway, Sweden or Jutland etc. This is a bit like people today referring to everyone from Asia as 'Indians', without specifying which country in Asia they originate from.

[2] Some Saxon deities give us the names of some of our days of the week: Tiwsday, Wodensday, Thorsday, Friggaday and Saetereday. (Sunday and Monday refer to the Sun and Moon.)

[3] For a more detailed and specific look at these beliefs, I can recommend *Wights and Ancestors* (Blain, 2000).

[4] Iceland was not converted to Christianity until about 1000 CE, much later than most other Western countries. Because there was still strong belief in the old religion, it was kept on as a second recognised national religion for use in private

only. In 1973 the idea of dual faith was legally re-affirmed through the work of Sveinbjorn Beinteinsson, and so one may be legally married by an Asatru gothi in Iceland today.

[5] Magic did not cease in Iceland with its Christianisation in 1000 CE. Some more recent magical spells are detailed in *The Galdrabók* (Flowers, 1989).

[6] Pennick (1994) suggests that the *ve* (pronounced *vay*) was originally triangular.

[7] This term *fylga* is sometimes confused with *hamingja*. Basically, a *fylga* is thought to be a projection of the person's own being, while a *hamingja* is an exterior personal guardian spirit, sometimes acting on the person's behalf.

[8] Some independent Odinists have just built the first new heathen temple for over 1000 years in another privately owned wood just north of London. Traditionally, the Norse and Anglo-Saxon peoples celebrated their spirituality both in the hall, and at special hillside altars called *heargs* or *harrows*.

Chapter 10
Shamanism

A Pagan world is one of endless connection and communication between the individual and the inter-related, growing, changing, always evolving world that that person lives in. (MacLellan, 1997)

What is a Shaman?

'Shaman' and 'Shamanism' are over-used words, and have developed modern meanings far beyond those originally attached to them. The word 'Shaman' is of Russian origins, relating to the Tungus people of Eastern Siberia. There is a related Sanskrit word meaning someone who follows a particular path of religious discipline. Although the word was originally applied to a specific culture, it has been found that very similar systems of belief and methodology can be found in many other cultures, from the Native Americans (North and South), Anglo-Saxons, Norse and Celts, through to Africans, Australian Aborigines and most peoples in between. While some of those cultures may have learnt to be what Joan Halifax (1979) termed 'technicians of the sacred and masters of ecstasy' from each other, it seems that many others developed these skills in isolation. Inevitably, they have developed their own independent terminology to describe what they do, and may not call themselves Shamans, such as the Polynesian-derived *Kupua* of Hawaii.

Shamans – whom we in the 'civilized' world have called 'medicine men' and 'witch doctors' – are the keepers of a remarkable body of ancient techniques that they use to achieve and maintain well-being and healing for themselves and members of their communities. These Shamanic methods are strikingly similar the world over, even for peoples whose cultures are quite different in other respects, and who have been separated by oceans and continents for tens of thousands of years. (Harner, 1980)

At its most basic level, a Shaman (male or female) is someone who goes into a trance state to travel psychically within the spirit world. While there, magical action may be attempted with the aid of 'power animals' or spiritual guides. The relationship with these helpers is maintained by careful respect and regular dialogue. Frequently this supernatural action is to cure disease, which the Shaman sees as mainly caused by spiritual means. In most cases it is the Shaman who takes the drug, not the patient, although occasionally they may both take it together. Whatever the method, a Shaman gets judged on results, and thus will depend very much on the spread of a good reputation. That is as relevant today as it was in the past, and people are more likely to turn to an old established successful (yet often humble) Shaman than any new and flashier practitioner with no proven track record.

Traditional Shamans, while often knowledgeable about herbal remedies, massage, and other treatments, see most illnesses as having spiritual causes. But even the modern Pagan community is ambivalent toward this idea as demonstrated by our actions when sick: whether with herbs or antibiotics we primarily treat symptoms. (Clifton, 1994)

One of the problems facing a modern Shaman is that their patients are unlikely to make a direct connection between spiritual belief and medicine. Furthermore, the Native American Shaman (and others) may label what he does for people as 'medicine', but if we examine it we find that it is more likely to resemble magic than the prescriptions we obtain from mainstream Western physicians.

In a larger perspective, Indian medicine encompasses much more than medical beliefs and practices. It is indeed a whole socioreligious complex that takes in many different cultural facets, as is the case in most countries. (Hultkrantz, 1997)

The Methods

Typically, traditional Shamans are recognised as suitable for training while still young. This training is likely to be mainly experiential. It is said that a Shaman walks between two worlds, this one and the 'other' world. Imagine the difficulties you would face if you tried to tell a primitive tribesman about New York, when he had no concept of buildings, electricity, cars or work. That is the difficulty faced by Shamans trying to discuss what they do, whether it be to an apprentice or a social anthropologist.

> We are like magnets calling events towards us according to our inner beliefs and 'dreams'. Dream it with strongly focussed intent, as Shamans do, and the universe will respond. (Rutherford, 1996)

Sometimes part of the training experience may make the trainee very sick, or even close to death, when they are subjected to hallucinogenic plants and fungi. This is often thought necessary, as a sort of death and rebirth experience. Fasting for a period can also induce a light-headed hallucination, although one must be aware of the physical, medical limitations and not exceed them. For example, they would be a complete non-starter if, like me, you were diabetic! Other times physical exhaustion and fear can be used to jolt the trainee out of their mundane world:

> He pointed out that after I had run up the hill for dear life I was in a perfect state for 'stopping the world'. Combined in that state were fear, awe, power and death; he said that such a state would be pretty hard to repeat. I whispered into his ear, "What do you mean by 'stopping the world?'" He gave me a ferocious look before he answered that it was a technique practised by those who were hunting for power, a technique by virtue of which the world as we know it was made to collapse. (Castaneda, 1972)

In some cultures, the Shaman is someone who has some sort of disability; this is sometimes termed 'the wounded healer' principle, in that it is believed that a person cannot heal others if they have not been injured themselves. Sometimes differences such as being an albino or homosexual may mark one out as 'different' and suitable for the path. Howard G Charing of Eagle's Wing claims to have had a transformational experience after a serious lift crash accident.

Trance States

Trance states can be arrived at by various means. Some Shamans dance themselves to a state of hyperventilating exhaustion, and one can understand why the term 'Shamanic' has been used to describe the ecstatic states of dancers within the 'rave culture' of modern dance music. Of course, those dancers may also utilise drugs such as ecstasy or LSD, and this has some parallels with Shamans. The main difference though is that Shamans try to control their intake of hallucinogens to achieve a particular goal. Those substances may be peyote (a South American cactus, mentioned in the works of Carlos Castaneda), magic mushrooms (Sami and Anglo-Saxons), ayahuasca (upper Amazon),[1] alcohol (Caribbean) or various types of tobacco and incense (Native Americans).

Repetitive chanting or drumming is also a tool used by many to achieve a higher (or lower) plane of consciousness. Additionally a rattle or bells attached to the clothing of a dancer may be used. Some Shamans (particularly Native Americans and Australians in their 'Dream Time') sing a monotonous, lengthy song, which will vary from tribe to tribe. Nowadays it is known that the brain can 'lock onto' certain frequency rhythms, a fact utilised by the makers of hi-tech dance music who are very particular about the 'beats per minute', and the regulations regarding strobe lighting. I have noticed that in half-light or in the dark (especially by a bonfire) the regular beat of a drum is often accompanied by a flashing produced by the motion of the stick and the skin of the drum catching the light. As a drummer I have experienced becoming entranced while beating out a steady pattern of beats. It is almost like a form of self-hypnosis, similar to that which I describe in my book *Pathworking* (Jennings and Sawyer, 1993).[2]

Physical pain can also be used to induce altered states of conscious. I am thinking specifically of the body piercing rituals of some Native Americans, among others, but would also apply this to the tattoos and other body piercing practised by various cultures around the world. Whether it is having a tattoo, incised scarring, piercing the body for jewellery, insertion of bones, hanging by a hook through the skin or whatever, the body has its own internal processes for dealing with pain, with the brain releasing powerful chemicals to block it out. These can result in a euphoric, delirious state, sometimes also experienced by victims of serious injury. Many of my friends who have had tattoos have become quite addicted to the process, while admitting the pain involved. To a certain extent this is another form of chemical-induced trance, but using chemicals naturally occurring within the body. While not recommending causing yourself (or anyone else) physical pain, one has to admit that this is a method adopted by many Shamans historically.

Finally, there is the sweat lodge, particularly associated with some Native American practices but also popular elsewhere. These sauna-like steam rooms should also be approached with caution, and at least one British person has died from the effects of becoming too dehydrated and short of breath in such a place. It is important always to make sure that it is properly set up and that there is no pressure exerted to stay beyond one's physical capabilities.

> Entering naked into the body of the turtle places us in the primeval state before birth as we sit inside the body of our mother. At the centre of the lodge sits a pit full of red-hot rocks, just like the hottest part of the earth lies in its central core of magma. From it flows the cleansing steam, just like cleansing and nourishing blood flows from our hearts and from the heart of Grandmother Earth. In the darkness we can lose ourselves, meet with the insubstantial, and participate in the unconscious reality, which permeates all of creation. In Shamanic activity the mythic is experienced, and the impossible can be felt. We must be prepared to feel the impossible. (Greg Stafford, quoted in Jones and Matthews, 1990)

What Makes a Shaman?

While training and experience are very important, many recognised leaders in the field emphatically make the point that living the life, banging a drum, going into trances, and so on, do not make you a Shaman. As Gordon MacLellan said at the 1999 Pagan Federation National Conference: 'You are only a Shaman when you are serving someone else as being one. Courses, clothing and fancy tools count for nothing without that.'

Similarly, Leo Rutherford (1996) says that a Shaman is 'someone who has fully walked the path of transformation and chosen to become a healer, helper, seer, prophet, in service to the people.' Howard G Charing of the same Eagle's Wing organisation adds: 'Shamanism is not Shamanism if done in isolation.'

This emphasises the integral community aspect of Shamanism, yet it is essentially a solitary path beyond its training. There are various sources of training for people not living within a Shamanic culture, although there are always reservations voiced by those who find it difficult to envisage it being effective for anyone raised in a highly developed urban culture. Of all the Pagan paths that one may pursue, I believe that Shamanism is the most likely to turn one's life upside down, and should therefore not be entered into lightly.

Many Pagans say that they sometimes utilise Shamanic methods. One might query their definition of what constitutes 'Shamanic', and I would suggest that it is very difficult to casually utilise methods of a system that requires such total self-immersion, alteration of perceptions and long-term personal change and growth. Facing a Shamanic journey requires a special sort of courage, and a willingness to take responsibility for whatever truths one discovers on it.

> You should only go looking for Vision if you are prepared to follow the Vision that speaks to you. (MacLellan, 1999)

Western Shamanism

With anthropologists only recently starting to explore the world of Shamanism within more exotic cultures than our own, it is not surprising that initially many Pagans interested in this field were drawn to the more easily accessible systems of the Native Americans and Siberians. For many, their sole source of information was the series of popular books by Carlos Castaneda describing South American Shamanism in the early 1970s. However, some notable writers dealing with Saxon Shamanism opened up the field in the 1980s and 1990s. The psychologist Brian Bates initially incorporated his academic findings into a novel, *The Way of Wyrd* (1983), which gives a splendidly intuitive feeling of what it must have been like to encounter an Anglo-Saxon Shaman. He later followed the book up with the more straightforward factual *The Wisdom of Wyrd* (1996). His work was acknowledged with a professorship at Sussex University in England. The *Wyrd* referred to in both titles is the Norse and Saxon concept of a giant web, interconnecting every person and incident. Any action at any point will cause tremors and knock-on effects at all other points, meaning that all fates are interwoven, and one decision can affect many other disparate issues.

> That is the way of the Wyrd. Events flow in cycles like the tides of the oceans. (Bates, 1983)

The Wyrd Sisters (as in the witches in Shakespeare's *Macbeth*), or the Fates, decide the past, present and future, spinning, weaving and

cutting the thread of life for each person. They are known as the
Norns in Norse belief, bearing the names of Urd, Verdandi and
Skuld, which mean Fate, Necessity and Being respectively.

> Life-force permeates everything. It is the source of all vitality. In a
> person it is generated in the head, flows like a stream of light into the
> marrow of the spine and from there into the limbs and crevices of
> the body. Power-plants help to control the channels through which the
> energy flows. (Bates, 1983)

I sometimes think that the one characteristic that is shared by genuine Shamans is a childlike sense of wonder at the natural and spiritual world. In treading their perilous path they seem to display a joy
of consciously living life to the full enhanced by living on its edge.

> Life is wonderful. To be alive is a wonder. To be a conscious part of the
> endless, spreading web of connections that links everything together is a
> celebration. For me 'magic' is working within that awareness, with a
> knowledge of being a part of all that is, touching threads that also weave
> into all that has been and reach, unravelling, into what might yet be. That
> web may be the energy and dynamics of physics or the remorseless wave
> of evolution, it may be the Wyrd, the Old Gods or the hand of God.
> Whatever it is, to work in it, with it and for it makes all of life a ceremony
> and a celebration. If that is not 'sacred', I do not know what is.
> (MacLellan, 1997)

The penultimate sentence of that quotation never fails to remind me
of that phrase from *The Wind in the Willows* when Ratty speaks of
his love of being on the river, 'by it, and with it, and on it, and in it.'
It is easy to become bogged downed in the serious nature of our
beliefs, and I think we all occasionally need reminding of the joy and
glory of being alive and aware of our magical world. For me, the
flower that defiantly forces itself through a crack in a concrete slab
to blossom briefly is as magical an event as any amount of knife-
waving in a circle.

The American academic Michael Harner wrote the engrossing
Way of the Shaman (1980). Alongside this, studies into the religious
practices of the Norse peoples, particularly in Iceland, revealed a
superb description of a visiting Shamanic seeress to a community.[3]
Although some of the elements of what we associate with Shamanism
elsewhere are not mentioned in this recount, the process is described
by most writers as Shamanistic, which illustrates how hard the term
is to define. This also leads us into the idea that a Shaman may use

whatever is necessary to effect a cure, including herbal remedies, psychological sleight of hand, ritual, talismans and fetish objects. Harner (1980) describes the clear practice of transference magic, with Sioux Indians transferring unhappiness into tobacco, and Coast Salish Indians becoming a protected pseudo-patient for the transference of illness from another of their community, exchanging clothes and acting in empathy with the patient's outlook.

The Shaman 'Artos', writing in the *Pagan Dawn* magazine, succinctly summarised the ideas given to me by several modern Shamans, concerning the similarities and differences between Shamanism and Wicca:

> My given path, that of a Shaman, is lonely, and Wiccan-based practices, open to all, can be shared with every genuine traveller who follows their own unique and individual journey to their spiritual centre. We are one: we are many. We all find our way, moving in the general direction of green spirituality, polytheism, animism and self-development. We share the same basic beliefs and activities that are outside mundane time and space. Ours is the world of the sacred, though in a busy life many may not have the time to explore it until they are older and can truly follow the way of the spiritual warrior . . . Shamanism has to be felt. It is carried on inside people and changes with them, but the contact, the tie with the land, is constant. Writings are not as adaptable, but frozen in time and space.

Things to do

- You may not have access to a sweat lodge, but have you ever tried a sauna? It is not the same, but can give you a rough idea of what one is physically like, especially if it is darkened or if you keep your eyes closed.

References

[1] Harner (1980) vividly describes his perceptions after trying the liquid distilled from certain vines and leaves with the Coinibo people of Peru. Its alternative names are the 'soul vine' and 'little death', which from the text seem very apt.

[2] Pathworking is a process of making creative visualisations by meditational techniques. It is a very popular, easy and simple tool for many Pagans and others. I do not personally class it as Shamanistic, as the scenarios are set artificially, and do not require a deep trance but only light relaxation, and the practitioner remains conscious and in control.

[3] From the Saga of Erik the Red.

Chapter 11

Male and Female Mystery Groups and Psychic Questers

A group of women in a feminist Witchcraft coven once told me that, to them, spiritual meant 'the power within oneself to create artistically and change one's life.' These women saw no contradiction between their concern for political and social change and their concern for 'things of the spirit', which they equated with the need for beauty or with that spark that creates a poem or a dance.

(Adler, 1986)

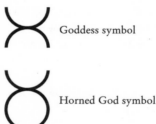

Goddess symbol

Horned God symbol

Female Mystery Groups

According to some sources, there was once a universal matriarchy and Goddess worship, which was later replaced and suppressed by aggressive, male, monotheistic religion. Personally the evidence submitted does not convince me, nor most academics. Much of the source of this belief comes from the popular source book by Robert Graves, *The White Goddess* (1948). According to Hutton (1991), it was written in a matter of weeks and Graves said to friends that it was what he wished for, rather than what had happened. He is also responsible for inventing a Celtic tree calendar and promoting a triple Goddess form. Having said that, I do believe that there was once a better balance of feminine deities, and that at least in some cultures women were held in higher esteem than in much later historical periods. For example, an Icelandic Pagan woman of 900 CE could divorce and own land and had legal protection and equal voting rights with male land-owners. It took the Suffragettes of Christian England until 1918 to regain even a fraction of those rights.

> In sociological terms women are a minority – our values and attitudes are secondary to the prevailing view, therefore women are inclined to under-value themselves as they have formerly looked outside themselves for an estimation of their value. When we look to masculine imagery we rarely see reality because the view is often stylised, fantasised, unrealistic or worse still derogatory, added to which women are normally viewers of culture rather than makers of it. (Lynne Morgan, cited in Harvey and Hardman, 1996)

With the increased emphasis on equal rights for women during the second half of the twentieth century, it was inevitable that women would look for equality in their spiritual lives as well as in the area of work and relationships. In the new liberated age of the late 1960s and early 1970s, this quest coincided with the publication and popularity of Witchcraft and Paganism. With a discovery that there were Goddesses and priestesses as well as Gods and priests, it is hardly surprising that the women who had felt oppressed by the major world religions should embrace this newly available spirituality whole-heartedly. When they also found that the priestess was often regarded as the ascendant, and that female sexuality was celebrated, not shunned, their enthusiasm was understandable, but the attraction of non-hierarchical female leaders has not been with-out its problems:

> The issue of leadership has plagued the feminist movement and the New Left. Exemplars of power-from-within are sadly lacking on the American political scene. Power-over-others is correctly seen to be oppressive, but too often the 'collective ideal' is misused, to tear down the strong instead of to build strength in the weak. Powerful women are attacked instead of supported. (Starhawk, 1979)

Some of that enthusiasm resulted in women being keen to join mixed-gender covens. While some found fulfilment there, others found that not all Pagan groups were free of patriarchal attitudes, and therefore went and formed female-only groups. Because many of these groups chose Diana as their principal Goddess, they became known as Dianics. Some of these groups are female only, while others allow male membership, so long as they are happy to be part of Goddess-based spirituality, as opposed to a balance of male and female divinities. Some female-only groups are quite militantly political (especially in the USA), while others are of a quieter nature, happy to form a supportive sisterhood, with an abhorrence of any form of hierarchy or dogma.

The merging of spiritual with political agendas has been viewed as disturbing by some sectors of the Pagan movement, who are in the main quite cynical about politics and politicians, particularly as their workings are often seen as hierarchical and not helpful to Paganism. Whether you share this view depends on whether you are optimistic enough to believe change is possible from within the system or as pessimistic as the person who wrote the slogan 'Don't vote for politicians; it only encourages them.'

Free of male opinion and sensitivities, many groups give extra focus to female-centred rites of passage, such as the start and ending of menstruation. Many are inspired by such writers as Starhawk (1979), Budapest (1990), Sjoo and Mor (1991) and Estes (1998), and are often quite influential within the wider world of feminist issues. These groups are often hard to find, and form a very small, but important and influential, part of the range of Pagan paths.

> Where women have felt themselves oppressed by the structures of patriarchal society, they have been eager not to emulate and reproduce those structures in their own religious movements. Women's traditions are therefore often eclectic and loose structured. Creativity and spontaneity are strongly encouraged; as is free emotional expression. The emphasis in women's groups is on immanent power – power from within. (Crowley, 1995)

Male Mystery Groups

Having been challenged by the new-found confidence of feminists, there was a period (which some may say still lingers) of the male in retreat, uncertain of his role or how to act in a changed world. While some men learnt to adapt and revise their opinions of the role of women, for others there was a defensive backlash and a re-asserting of macho behaviour and values. Many Pagan males have taken the situation as a positive opportunity instead. While there is still a feeling of guilt about how men have historically mistreated women and the world in general, there is a current of thought expressing itself in wanting to use male strength in positive ways.

Being allowed to be creative, show feelings and cry, to have an equal, non-dependent partnership with a female, and to bond with other males without necessarily being thought homosexual, were liberating ideas for many. In the USA, it was often gay men (sometimes under the banner 'Radical Faeries') who were the original movers and shakers, just as the female mysteries groups were often started by lesbians or bisexuals. The nature of the movement however does not appear to be of any specific sexual preference. Inspired by books such as *Iron John* (Bly, 1999) and *The Way of Merlin* (Stewart, 1991), they organised male-only camps and activities where they could rediscover and rebuild themselves. While not all of these projects were specifically Pagan, many were, and the kindred spirits that met there subsequently formed male-oriented spiritual groups, which would endeavour to put into practice the teachings and experiences they had received. Some are particularly focused on these two texts, or may try to identify with the Green Man, Pan or Cernunnos. Once again, these groups are few in number and hard to find, but are nevertheless an important strand of modern Paganism.

Access to Male and Female Mystery Groups

You may more easily find both male and female mystery groups through New Age shops and magazines than through more Pagan mainstream outlets. Most are very localised, and do not belong to any form of national organisation. Some have closed membership, since they have established a group of people with whom they feel comfortable and do not wish to risk altering the dynamics. If you are really keen, and cannot find one, you may have to start one yourself from networks of like-minded friends.

Psychic Questers

This is a sub-group on the fringe of Paganism, containing members of many different traditions, as well as some people (such as psychics and mediums) outside of them. Psychic Questers use a variety of skills and disciplines to solve esoteric mysteries, including dowsing, intuition, trance, literary research, spiritual mediumship, ritual, divination and pure detective work. Sometimes they are seeking a particular historic artefact, or knowledge of a special place or magical subject. Some believe they are in direct competition with darker forces such as Satanists, who will try to thwart them. Opinions about their authenticity are strongly divided, but many Pagans have read the books by, or are aware of, people such as Andrew Collins (1988), who have a strong following. Also influential in this field is the book *The Holy Blood and the Holy Grail* (Baigent, Leigh and Lincoln, 1996).

Things to do

- Get a sheet of paper and divide it into two columns, headed 'male' and 'female'. Now in the male column list some positive characteristic terms commonly associated with men, such as *manly*, *ambitious*, *stud*. Opposite these terms, write down what you think they become when applied to women, such as *tomboy*, *social climber*, *slut*. Now do the same in reverse. For example, for women: *feminine*, *intuitive*, *attractive*; and for men: *effeminate*, *a dreamer*, *a dandy*. Do you see how we make value judgements about behaviour, depending whether the person exhibiting it is male or female?

- Whatever your gender, try doing one physical activity traditionally associated with the opposite sex. For men this may be arranging a vase of flowers, bathing a child or baking a cake. For women, it could be checking the oil level of a car, chopping firewood or even playing football. Afterwards, think about how it made you feel doing it, and whether if given the choice you would want to change sex.

Chapter 12
Eclectic Paganism and Foreign Traditions

A thing well said will be wit in all languages.
(John Dryden)

Eclecticism

With so many different Pagan paths and their myriad variations, it is not surprising that a number of Pagans never settle on one particular mythology and methodology. Some may do this due to indecisiveness, or because they are taking their time and are still searching for the one that meets their requirements and aspirations. Others make it a deliberate policy, saying that as all paths are but different aspects of the same truths, it does not matter how you label your beliefs or what sort of structure you put them into; it is better to take the most useful and appealing elements from several cultural sources. We have already seen that this has happened within some modern developments of Wicca, but it also applies to general Paganism.

Inevitably, there are also others who decry the practice, and term it 'pick and mix', alleging that such people are avoiding the elements of each path that are harder to get to grips with, and showing disrespect by only selecting the more attractive features. Some of the original practitioners have been critical as well in recent years; some Native Americans have objected to the perceived cultural imperialism of white men 'ripping off' aspects of their culture such as dreamcatchers, while not appreciating the complex set of beliefs attached to them. I myself have publicly attacked the use of runes as a fortune-telling toy by those entirely ignorant of their spiritual context within the Norse and Anglo-Saxon cultures.

In some ways, the Eclectic Pagan or Wiccan is a relatively modern phenomenon. Although many belief systems start out as an amalgam of parts of others, once they have found, established and developed their own form, they may stay fairly rigid for a long period, particularly when the adherents have little or no contact with other belief systems. For a long time it was difficult enough to find a single coven to become attached to, and to learn their ways. Covens kept strictly apart, partly through a fear of a breach of confidentiality and, in a few cases, to protect the leader's position as the unquestionable fount of all knowledge. With the legalising of Witchcraft, and people more able to declare their Pagan spirituality openly, the situation changed. Magazines, moots and conferences (and more latterly the Internet) present a plethora of opportunities to compare, debate and challenge beliefs and practice, something which most Pagans relish as free thinkers.

Public group rituals have had to cater for and accommodate a wide range of religious attitudes, either by taking mutually acceptable elements from several practices, or forming completely new ones, suitable for a large crowd to participate in. Occasionally this can lead to the blandness of the 'lowest common denominator', but more often the creativity of Pagans has ensured that these rituals are just as wonderful as smaller, discreet affairs. As someone who occasionally writes and leads such rituals, I will readily admit to conducting them in a different way. In particular, the small nuances of a change in vocal tone or moving of one's hand is lost to a larger crowd, so there is a need to be more theatrical and more flamboyant in style. It is not unknown at large rituals to have a whole band of musicians, lighting effects, public address system, giant bonfire, chanting and drumming, food and drink, choreographed dancers and a carefully rehearsed ritual drama in costume, complete with fog machine! This will frequently be designed to act upon all five senses (sight, hearing, taste, touch and smell) and involve the crowd as participants (singing, dancing, chanting, etc.) rather than observers. Inevitably, some of that crowd will want to take some of those ideas home with them to incorporate into the practices of their local group.

One can understand the critics who say that all the individual traditions will end up as one homogeneous mass if this is allowed to go unchecked by the Elders of each path, and that it is important for Pagans to have some personal core beliefs and practices. There is always a danger through peer pressure in feeling that you must go along with the crowd. I have been to events where I did not agree with the emphasis or content of chants, for instance, in which case I simply refrained from joining in, but others might feel that they are expected to participate fully.

Countering that, others say it is a healthy practice, preventing group leaders from becoming over-powerful, the paths from becoming irrelevant or moribund, and that only practices that are no longer appropriate will ever be dropped. For some people not part of local groups, this will be their only opportunity to experience Pagan group ritual. They might find a small local group, practising in a quiet, meditative way, too tame by comparison, and would prefer to keep the option of practising in a variety of ways.

Meanwhile I will offer the impish thought that one of the most structured forms of Wicca, Gardnerian, was eclectic in its inception. Gardner drew material from Rosicrucians, Traditionals, The Key of Solomon book, Doreen Valiente, Aleister Crowley and others, as well as using his own ideas in creating a modern Pagan orthodoxy.

Foreign Traditions

Of course, there are also those who take on board a complete spiritual system, but one not readily associated with their own country. There are many Pagans who have a fascination with the religion of Ancient Egypt, or of the Native American, South American or Haitian Voodoo Shaman. For some, it may be because they have an ancestral connection, or believe they were earlier incarnated in one of those regions. Others will openly admit that they have no direct connection to their area of interest, but are genuinely and deeply attracted to it. For some this can have expensive or traumatic consequences, such as emigrating to the land of attraction or making frequent expensive trips. A good example of this is those who frequently take themselves off to Egypt, Greece or Rome to wander among the ancient tombs and temples and, if they are lucky, actually celebrate rites there. However, in doing so they may well upset local opinion, which may not be as tolerant of the older religions of their native country. In some cases these travellers are following in the footsteps of the Victorian occultists who were dazzled and fascinated by the treasures that were unearthed in Egypt and elsewhere. They often had much easier access to these foreign belief systems than they did to British Witchcraft, which was still illegal at that time.

One of the added attractions to such a path (apart from the thrill of the exotic) is the fact that often far more is known about these religious practices than our own. One can study the Egyptian Book of the Dead (complete with its invocations and magical instructions) and lots of other hieroglyphic texts or read many first-hand accounts of Greek and Roman Paganism, either in the original text or in translation. Imagine if we could access the same sort of information and do the same for Druidry or other paths! Of course, one may also find that foreign Pagan beliefs are not that different to our native ones, despite the differences in names and artefacts.

One could argue that most of the British Pagan belief systems are foreign in origin anyway, since the Celts, Romans, Saxons and Norse were all immigrants or conquerors. Apart from Hindu and Sikh immigrants who, with their multitude of nature deities, practise major Pagan religions in their own right, following a foreign Pagan path is always likely to be a minority area of UK Paganism by its very nature, but an important sector none the less.

Things to do

- You may not be able to travel to exotic places abroad, but you could experience a foreign nature religion by visiting a local Hindu temple. I have found that they are friendly places, only too delighted to explain their religious beliefs and answer your questions, especially if you show a respect for their sacred place.

- Why not read a book about an unfamiliar mythology such as Egyptian, Roman or Native American? Can you find similarities with more familiar belief systems, or can it teach you a different way of viewing things?

Chapter 13
Magical Theory and its Ethics

Magic is the science of the control of the secret forces of nature. (SL MacGregor Mathers, Chief of the Order of the Golden Dawn, cited in Valiente, 1993)

```
A B R A C A D A B R A
 A B R A C A D A B R
  A B R A C A D A B
   A B R A C A D A
    A B R A C A D
     A B R A C A
      A B R A C
       A B R A
        A B R
         A B
          A
```

What is Magic?

It is interesting to note that Mathers termed Magic a science, contrary to most other leading figures describing it as 'an Art' or 'the Craft'. Crowley hedged his bets:

> The science and art of causing Change to occur in conformity with Will. (quoted in Farrar, 1990)

Ronald Hutton offers Sir James Frazer's definition:

> Practices designed to bring spiritual or supernatural forces under the control of human agents. (Hutton, 2000)

This older viewpoint of magicians bringing forces 'under control' is worth highlighting. I believe it has echoes of the Alchemist and Cabbalist 'commanding' spirits and demons to do their bidding, and subjugating them. A more modern outlook would appear to appeal to benevolent forces, rather than threaten them, although regrettably I must admit I rarely hear the word 'please' used in ritual. I have always thought it worth being polite to someone more powerful of whom you are asking a favour. I sometimes think the defining factor is if a magician uses a circle to confine a supernatural force rather than to welcome it.

Many occultists divide the field into 'High Magic' and 'Low Magic'. High Magic is said to be that of trying to bring about the spiritual enlightenment or personal development of the practitioner, and a closer relationship and understanding of the Divine Cosmos. Low Magic is more concerned with the mundane and everyday world, and includes spells for healing, gaining wealth, position or a partner, as well as magic to aid environmental campaigns. Many, but not all, believe that magic should not be used to gain personal wealth. I can assure you that there are very few wealthy Pagans, so that is probably correct. However, instead of doing a spell for a shiny new sports car, one could in Higher Magic do a spell to remove the personal longing within you for that sports car.

Does Magic Work?

Of course there are all sorts of theories as to whether magic works, and if so, how. There is the cynic's argument that the outcome required would have happened anyway, or that it is more the result of practical action than any magic. Since most of us try to do things practically before using magic, it would be difficult to separate this out. Coincidence is another valid argument, although in my experience some of the results I have seen would be most unlikely to have happened by chance. People arguing for the success of magic will inevitably quote incidences of when it appears to have worked, but it is only fair to ask how many times they report failure. The law of averages must give some positive results without any outside agency being involved.

I once tried to help a friend caught up in problems with a suspected fraudulent will. Much depended on the individual suspected of fraud making a statement to a solicitor confirming it was genuine. Past experience had made us expect he would have no scruples about this. I did some magic to spur his conscience into action. Over the course of the next two months, he was found out to be a liar by several people who had in the past been taken in frequently by his charming ways. Afterwards they talked about him being permanently confused, tripping himself up by telling conflicting lies to the same person, not a mistake he had ever made in previous years. Furthermore, he continually delayed signing and sending back the statement prepared by the solicitor. I had not specified how he should be prevented in his fraudulent claims, only that he should be aware of his conscience, which I felt was within my code of ethics.

People who attempt to work magic (and I include myself in that group) generally say that they do not know how it works, but it very often does, and frequently in quite peculiar and unexpected ways. Certainly there are theories about thoughts being projected, or divine intervention by the spiritual entities they have appealed to, but most people are more interested in the results than dissecting the process. Most will admit to it not being an exact science, but rather an uncertain art. Inevitably magic relies upon an act of faith by its practitioners, but not necessarily from its beneficiaries. As Eliphas Levi (1913) says in *The History of Magic*:

> Magic combines in a single science that which is most certain in philosophy with that which is eternal and infallible within religion. It reconciles perfectly and incontestably those two terms so opposed on the first view – faith and reason, science and belief, authority and liberty.

I was interested to hear an item on the radio about a year ago. An atheist doctor was working at an American hospice for patients who were very ill. He noticed that some patients who were visited by their church groups and prayed for seemed to have a better recovery and survival rate. He tried an experiment. He created three groups of patients. The first had no spiritual beliefs or help. Christian friends prayed for the second and the third group had non-Christians including Buddhist, Hindu and Humanists think positive thoughts about them. He also created a control group who thought they were being prayed for, but were not.

The control group and the group who knew that they were getting no spiritual help had almost identical recovery rates. What he found more surprising was that the other two groups both had very similar recovery rates, which were about 20 per cent higher than the rest of those studied. As a result, the doctor has since become a non-specific religious person, and is continuing his experiments. Like the magicians, he cannot understand how it works, but is convinced that it does.

It would be good to see some independent, unbiased research on the efficacy of magic in the future. Unfortunately, it is not an area likely to stimulate much academic interest or funding, which is a shame when it is of interest to so many people. By its very nature it defies most scientific analysis, and it is always difficult to prove whether a required outcome happens by magic, by coincidence or by psychology. To explain that, let me quote one more example, from a coven of Witches in the North of England. One of their female members fell out with a woman whom she knew through taking their children to school together. After the argument, the woman started telling lies about her former friend, claiming that she was sexually promiscuous. She also exposed her as a Witch, a fact that had been kept hidden until then from the rest of the community. Upset, the Witch appealed to her directly to stop, but to no avail. Asking her coven for help, they came up with a magical plan. It so happened that the Witch had one of the gossip's old shopping lists, which she had been given with a telephone number on the back. They took this scrap of paper to form a magical link to the gossip. A small clay poppet (a term to describe a magical doll figure, whether it be made of wood, clay or whatever) was made and named to represent her, and the paper was placed inside. Within a ritual, a small scrap of red material was tied around the head where the mouth was scratched on, and a general request for her to stop telling lies was made. No particular action was specified as to how this was to be achieved.

The next day the gossip woke up with laryngitis, and could barely manage a hoarse whisper. After a couple of days she approached her former friend and croakily asked her to forgive her. Although she did not directly ask her to remove a spell, it seemed evident that she believed there was a connection. Graciously, the Witch agreed, saying her voice would soon get better, which it did the following day, after the coven had removed the gag from the poppet. Not long after, the woman moved away from the area, but not before some of the other mums at the school gates had started showing a new friendliness towards the Witch!

One can, of course, put several interpretations on the fact of the woman losing her voice. It could have been coincidence – after all, lots of people lose their voices temporarily. It could have been that the medicine she took for the sore throat took a few days to work, or it could have been psychosomatic, with the woman's guilt and knowledge of her friend being a Witch contributing to her condition. The other possibility is that it could have been pure magic. It would be very difficult to obtain scientific proof of what had happened. Notice, though, the knock-on effects. The other mums make sure they are friendly towards the Witch; they cannot be sure whether Witchcraft was responsible, but stay friends just in case. Also, whether their magic was responsible or not, the coven members would believe it was, which would give them more confidence (and success) in further magical work, so the psychological impact would be two-fold. As far as the magical ethics of the affair goes, one can observe that the coven only did enough to stop the action, and did not seek any other form of retribution. Also, practical solutions had been sought before resorting to magic in that the woman had clearly been asked to stop.

'Black' and 'White' Magic

If you meet a Christian, do you ask him if he is a 'good' Christian or a 'bad' Christian? No, so why do people always ask if you are a black or white Witch? Despite many Pagans' love of balanced polarity (black/white, day/night, dark/light), magic is not exclusively good or bad, any more than Christians are as a group. Magic is most often a muddy grey, since we can rarely accurately predict (even with runes, Tarot and a crystal ball) what the ultimate consequences of our magical success will be. For that reason alone, I think it is very worthwhile to pause and think about what sort of magic we should attempt, and when. I believe that there should be some ethics connected to magical practice, although there are some people, both past and present, who believe that there should be no such limitations imposed upon them.

Ethics

The most frequently heard, popular ethical rule goes along the lines of 'An it harm none'. This is an excellent principle, but magic and its usage are so complex that inevitably situations bring about dilemmas. Even walking across a field tramples plants and insects, so the principle taken to its ultimate conclusion would leave us immobile.

Consider an act of magic done to stop bulldozers moving in to create a six-lane highway through valued woodland. Of course the spell sounds ethical, saving those lovely trees, animals, plants, and so on. But supposing the spell you do is entirely successful? The bull-dozer driver will be out of a job; who will feed his family? So even the most benign-sounding spells are likely to harm someone. Of course, you could argue that the spell doesn't harm the bulldozer driver because it forces him to seek a better way of life and career choice – but I will leave you to explain that to him!

The intention of the spell was good in principle, but all magic has a 'knock-on' effect, not all of which will be positive or can be fore-seen without some powerful divination, something I think should proceed most acts of magic. Another frequently quoted principle is that of the 'Law of threefold return', where it is believed that what-ever you do, good or bad, will be repaid three times. Nobody seems quite sure whether this repayment should be instant, slow release or even within another reincarnated lifetime. Nobody even seems to know why it is threefold. Why not sevenfold or ninefold? I have frequently challenged the Pagan community to prove the Law's provenance and existence before the 1950s birth of Gardnerian Wicca. It is not that I want to attack it – I might even enjoy the thought of that school bully getting three black eyes for every one he hands out – but such an absolute belief needs to be examined for origins and accuracy, rather than being blindly accepted.

Compare all of this to Aleister Crowley's 'Do what thou wilt shall be the whole of the law. Love is the law, love under will.' He was say-ing that you should only act upon your higher self (your 'true will'), which should be dominated by the force of love. He was not saying 'do as you like', attractive though that may seem. Despite being of two completely different backgrounds, I would argue that this is not so very different from the modern version of the Wiccan Rede:

> Eight words the Witches' Creed fulfil;
> If it harms none, do what you will. (Valiente, 1993)

Some people seem to have a spell for every occasion, whether created originally by themselves, or from someone else's book. A common one is the love charm. ('Oh, if only you could get that fellow at the bus stop to fancy me and ask me for a date – he is so cute!') I make it a personal rule to refuse such requests. For a start, if the poor chap does not know what is going on, you are invading his privacy, choices and destiny. He might be attached, gay or celibate, or even biding his time until other complications are out of the way. Rushing the process might ruin it. Getting a couple of people together seems such a nice thing to do, but it can have awful consequences. Supposing the guy is free of commitments and has a mutual attraction to the girl. Shouldn't giving them a gentle nudge be seen as an act of positive magic? But what if it works, they fall in love, get married, have a baby and then a year down the line he turns out to be a wife-beating philanderer? Would that be good clean 'white' magic now? The intention was good, but we cannot say the same for the outcome.

We should always seek out the practical solution before using magic. If it is a medical problem get a doctor, and for a legal one get a lawyer. For personal problems, those involved should resolve it between themselves or via a mediator or counsellor. Magic should be used as a last resort, not a first reaction. It is too powerful a tool to be brought out willy-nilly. Would you use a chainsaw to dead-head the roses? I would argue that magic is very akin to a chainsaw – too extreme for many delicate matters, and dangerous in the wrong hands or without taking adequate precautions and thinking through its use. Having said that, I believe that there's a case for using it to increase the success rate or speed of the practical solution already applied.

The 'chainsaw' concept is a valid one in other areas. If you believe that magic works, you have to believe it is a very powerful force. Play around with a chainsaw without protecting yourself and sticking to the safety rules, and you will get hurt. So it is with magic. You have the whole of your life to learn, so why rush it and make dangerous mistakes? Experienced magicians do not set up circles, invoke protection, plan meticulously, and so on, for the fun of it. They do it to protect themselves, their colleagues and to ensure that the spirit that enters the space is the one they specifically invited!

Magical power can become an obsession with some people, particularly if their mental state is fragile due to illness or the use of drugs or alcohol. Magic does have a negative effect on a small percentage of occultists, and in extreme cases has lead to incarceration in hospitals. The 'other' world may also affect a large number of people who have not invited it into their lives. The psychiatric hospitals have many patients who claim to hear voices. It is sometimes suspected that they may be people driven insane by psychic abilities that they cannot control. While it is nigh impossible to prove, it is a fact that psychiatric nurses have measured significant increases in agitation and suicide attempts during the period of the full Moon, giving some basis of underlying truth to the old term 'lunatic'.

Healing is an area in which people often think they can only be doing good ethical magic. Consider this scenario: a friend sprains his wrist. He has visited the doctor but also asks you, 'Can you make it heal quickly for me, please?' You agree, and because of his rapid recovery, he is able to keep an appointment for a game of tennis, where he makes the acquaintance of a man. As a result of that meeting, the man gains his trust and swindles him out of his life savings. You aided the speedier recovery, thus changing his fate, which might have decreed that he never met the swindler. The intention was good, and a practical solution sought first, but your interference cost him his savings. If you believe that all things happen for a purpose (as opposed to the Gods just liking a joke!), should you have become involved? And if you did, should you have asked what he was going to do if he got better sooner, and would he take personal responsibility for the consequences?

Someone once said, 'All magic has a price'. I believe that to be true, not just in terms of physical, mental or spiritual dissipation, but in terms of that knock-on effect, making ripples or vibrations within the Web of the Wyrd. The trouble is that magic is so much fun, so useful, so seductive, that it is hard to resist using it despite the drawbacks. It is therefore vital that within our ethical structures, whatever our path, we try to make allowance for that. In the case of the lovelorn girl, we can do a different spell, to give her the confidence to take control and responsibility of her own life so that she can ask the guy out, something far simpler and more obvious. It could still lead to far-reaching consequences, but at least the relationship could be more open, natural and honest as a result.

I believe also that there is certain hypocrisy within magic-making. In the Icelandic sagas of my own Asatru tradition, there are heroes who benefit from magical help, and nobody decries it. Elsewhere in the sagas other magicians are executed for their use of magic against heroes. The implication is that it is all right to use magic against someone who I think is bad, but they must not use it against me because I think I am good – hypocritical is a word that springs to mind.

Ultimately intention has to be part of the equation, as well as considering the eventual consequences. Is the intention ethical? Does it feel 'right' within you? Will it do harm to anyone or anything? Consider the differences between 'binding' someone against doing you harm, cursing them and setting up a psychic mirror to reflect their evil back at them. Would it be ethical to set up a 'mirror' if you warned them about it first?

Harmony with Nature

Whatever our Pagan paths, we all claim to be in tune with nature. That means we should make sure our magic is in tune with natural forces as well. Of course, a cynic might argue that if you only apply magic to things that would happen naturally anyway, how could you ever know if it was yourself or nature being effective? For me, magic works best when I take a natural process and encourage it to be stronger, or to alter its rate. We then descend into the thorny subject of what magic is, but I would agree with the definition of projecting one's will to alter the course of events on both a physical and spiritual plane.

Your spiritual path should enable you to seek out the very essence of your higher self's will, but as you are a child of nature, should not your true will be ethical and in tune with nature anyway? This is a very good reason for people not to get involved in magic until they have a good knowledge of both their spiritual path and their inner self. After all, one can be a Pagan without ever working magic at all.

That last point is frequently overlooked by many new Pagans and writers and lecturers on Paganism, who somehow assume that we should all be dancing round in circles, shouting weird things and waving our arms about. Our Pagan ancestors may have mostly believed in magic, but that does not mean to say that they all practised it. They may have chosen not to get involved with it, or alternatively got an 'expert' to do it for them. Likewise today, one can hold Pagan beliefs without being involved in magical work, although, of course, depending on your definition of magic, your personal spiritual growth can be defined as a magical act in itself. It can be very easy at a Pagan camp, conference or other event to submit to peer pressure to join in with a group ritual containing magical work. If you are in any doubt about the nature of a rite, it is always best to ask those leading it. They will usually be pleased to advise you whether it is a straight non-magical celebration, or whether magic is to be attempted. After all, they do not want anyone unhappy within their circle, as negativity is liable to adversely affect the outcome. Do not be afraid to ask questions – it is how we all find out things and add to our experience. Anyone who belittles you for doing so is not worth working with, since arrogance and elitism should have no part in our paths. As one of the so-called 'experts', I frequently ask questions of the priest and priestess before a ritual. Some might say that is how I acquired my 'expert' status. Providing you are not delaying the actual rite, my experience has been that most leaders will be only too happy to expound on the significance and content of what they are doing at great length, and will respect you more for being a person who questions rather than following blindly.

Things to do

- Think of a problem you have personally encountered, and write it down. Now list all the possible non-magical things you could do to try to solve it, or how it could resolve itself, however unlikely or ridiculous. For example, if next door's cat keeps coming into your garden and destroying the flowerbeds, your actions could range from spraying the area with a cat-repellant, to shooting it on sight, with many other alternatives in between, such as buying a dog to have in your garden, grassing over the flowerbeds, and so on. The situation could even resolve itself by either the cat dying naturally or the owner moving and taking it with him.

- You have just listed all the different ways that a spell might work. Now, if you had worked a general spell to 'stop that cat destroying my flower bed', which of those alternatives would have been within your personal code of ethics? If you did not specify that the cat was not to be harmed, magic might have resolved it by the cat being run over. How would that principle apply to your specific problem? You have just demonstrated to yourself why magic should always be very specific in the outcome required (as in 'be careful what you wish for') and why it is best to use magic lightly, if at all.

Chapter 14
Using Magic

If you are going to leap an abyss do not take two steps.
(Chinese proverb)

Aries	Taurus	Gemini	Cancer
Leo	Virgo	Libra	Scorpio
Sagittarius	Capricornus	Aquarius	Pisces

Types of Magic

This book does not set out to be a source of spells or rituals. Many of the books I have recommended in Chapter 17 do carry such material. However, if you can truly focus your whole will towards a magical end, and use whatever techniques you personally feel confident with, then that is likely to be as effective as anything else that someone else has written down. After all, that is what somebody else did before they wrote it.

Something that is often missing from magical books is analysis of what type of magic is being attempted, and what other types of approach may be available. Many paths use several types of magic, and to a degree the classifications I have detailed here overlap each other.

Imitative or Sympathetic Magic

It is thought that the cavemen practised this when they drew hunting scenes. The theory is that if I depict myself as being successful in this action in pictorial or ritual form, this will result in it happening in reality. This is not so different from modern techniques for accomplishing complex tasks, such as mock exams, practice interviews and repeatedly rehearsing physical manoeuvres needed on space exploration. 'The harder I practise, the luckier I become' is a phrase that springs to mind.

Transference Magic

One can transfer outwards or inwards magically. One can invoke a God or Goddess into one's own body; this is often known as invocation. It is usually considered unwise to attempt this without careful preparation and taking care firstly that the entity is the right one, and, secondly, will leave when you want it to.

Transference magic also includes wishing an ailment into an object that is placed in the ground to rot, or writing something that one wishes to destroy on a piece of paper and burning it. The poppet doll, so beloved of horror filmmakers, is also an example of this. Although very few contemporary Witches would stick pins in an effigy of their enemy, it is evident from the many examples found in museums around the country (especially the Museum of Witchcraft in Boscastle, Cornwall) that this was far more common in the eighteenth and nineteenth centuries. It is an aspect of Witchcraft that is not much talked about among practitioners today, but I believe we should be honest and admit that our history has a darker side, as do many other spiritual paths.

Intuitive or Shamanic Magic

This will invariably involve the practitioner getting into a trance state, through chanting, music, drugs, alcohol, starvation, hallucinogenic substances, pain, and so on. In their altered state of consciousness, they will then access the 'other' spiritual realms, sometimes using spirit totem power animals as helpers. Apart from classical Shamanism, a number of other belief systems utilise some of these methods, including seidr magicians within the Northern Tradition, Witches, Voodoo, Native American and Australian Aboriginal peoples.

The process is also very similar to that described as 'astral travelling' when the operator sends a 'fetch' (spirit alter ego) to various 'astral planes' to find information or heal sick spirits. These astral planes are like several layers (frequently seven) of higher consciousness. Some describe the journeying of their mind as completely free-form, while others describe a strict separation of levels that are possible for them to reach, and a silvery thread-like umbilical cord, which will draw them back to their body if it is disturbed while their spirit is wandering.

Talismanic Magic

Talismans can be made for one specific purpose, as opposed to general-purpose lucky amulets. Although this practice sometimes overlaps with Imitative Magic, there can be talismans made purely with magical symbols and correspondences. The materials can range from the organic (bones/feathers/wood/paper) through to metal and stone. Some may derive their magical properties through spells or through what has been inscribed onto them, while other objects such as hag stones (a stone with a natural hole through it) or a cast-off horseshoe can be seen as inherently magic without any other intervention.

Ceremonial Magic

Not all ceremonial magicians are Pagan, although many are. Some may be Christian or Jewish, but since the general view of this grouping is that all spiritual paths are elements of one great path and truth, such distinctions are frequently unimportant. Sometimes this area of activity is designated the Western Mystery (or Esoteric) Tradition. The magic depends on the careful preparation and repetition of ritual actions to achieve its goals, and attempts to cause change within the participants as well as the universe. By duplicating a set of conditions exactly, you build up a powerful sense of the process being 'right', and in concentrating on the minutiae, you become totally focused on the desired result to the exclusion of the mundane world.

It is not a cheap method to adopt, since the ritual equipment of many different robes, banners, wands, incenses, and so on, required is extremely expensive. Within the system, the four elements are represented as fire (wand), water (cup), air (dagger) and earth (pentacle). It often merges into the area of Cabbalistic Magic described below. Some of the better-known influential Ceremonial Magicians have been members of the OTO (*Ordo Templi Orientis*) and the Golden Dawn. I asked one practitioner why she followed this path and whether she found it restrictive compared with the usual idea of magic being 'wild and free'. She said:

> I needed the discipline of a formal training. The postal course I took was the right thing for me. The way we were trained was a mental approach, rather than emotional. After a while I needed to add things to it, but it is very important to have mental discipline to focus. It helps you meditate with enhanced concentration, and ultimately enables you to be wild and free.

The *Ordo Templi Orientis* (OTO) was formed in Germany in 1902, probably by Karl Kellner and Theodor Reuss. They claimed to draw influences from Masonry and the Knights Templar. They appointed Aleister Crowley to set up a British branch, and he in turn initiated Gardner into it. However, Gardner was only active for about a year. Two organisations claim to be the direct descendants of the original OTO in the UK. One is the OTO Caliphate and the other OTO Typhonian, headed nowadays by Kenneth Grant in the USA (1972), but there are many more offshoots around the world claiming origins either from within the UK or from Germany.

Both these organisations have suffered splits and are now subdivided into several splinter groups across the world. The magical system is sometimes referred to as Enochian, which the translator Mathers claimed to be the magical language developed by the Elizabethan court astrologer Dr Dee. Enoch is a character briefly referred to in Genesis in the Bible, and is thought by some to have become an angel on a higher spiritual plane.

The Hermetic Order of the Golden Dawn (OGD) was founded in 1887–8 by two members of the Masonic-derived *Societas Rosicruciana in Anglia*, called WR Woodman and William Westcott. This organisation was purely magical, and had no specific religious affiliations. Its members come from a variety of religious backgrounds. It also had connections with George Pickingill (see Chapter 3) and was influenced by the French left-wing ex-cleric and Freemason Eliphas Levi,[1] with his work on Cabbalistic and Egyptian texts. Levi also made influential studies of magical correspondences and the incorporation of Tarot symbology into magic. The poet WB Yeats was a member of the Golden Dawn (and wrote some of their rituals), as was the author AE Wait, who created the very popular Rider Waite Tarot pack. The OGD was also influenced by the writings of William Blake. Another leading member was Samuel Mathers (better known as MacGregor Mathers), who translated a number of old magical texts (including those of the Elizabethan Dr Dee, 1527–1608) and introduced Aleister Crowley into the Order, who in turn was much influenced by Allan Bennett (1872–1923). Israel Regardie, who was also a student of Crowley, succeeded Mathers in his work.

Other members included the authors Algernon Blackwood and Edith Nesbit, the actress Florence Farr, and Violet Firth (better known as Dion Fortune, 1890–1946). Dion Fortune started out as a member of the Golden Dawn, and went on to write some successful occult fiction, such as *The Sea Priestess* (1976), and founded the Fraternity of the Inner Light, which blended Pagan and Christian mysticism, for which she has been much criticised. Nowadays, the offshoot Oxford Golden Dawn Occult Society is a major influence on the UK esoteric scene, with frequent lectures, debates and conferences.

> Like the ancient Gnostics, whose teachings form one of the roots of the Golden Dawn system, Golden Dawn magicians aren't willing to settle for belief; they want to know. (John Michael Greer, Witchvox website)

Although many Golden Dawn magicians practise alone, those who work together in temples have a complex system of grades, noted here in ascending order. In the Outer Order there are: Neophyte, Zelator, Theoricus, Practicus and Philosophus. In the Inner Order there are: Portal, Adeptus Minor, Adeptus Major and Adeptus Exemptus. Higher symbolic grades: Magister Templi, Magus and Ipsissimus.

Thelemic Magic

Thelemic Magic is the main Magic practised by Aleister Crowley and the people he has influenced. One does not have to be a follower of Crowley to use Thelemic ideas, but he was its most prominent modern commentator and practitioner. *Thelema* is Greek for 'will', and Crowley claimed not to have invented the system but to have channelled it from psychic sources, and then written it down. It is really an amalgam of the many strands of magical current he studied in depth and developed, including much Eastern (particularly Egyptian) material, but also including Masonic ritual, Cunning Man Craft, Tantric Sex Magic and probably drug-induced Shamanism. It is usually described as a 'left-hand path', along with various other forms of ceremonial magic, as opposed to the 'right-hand path' of witches. These are terms thought more appropriate to classifying types of magic than 'black' or 'white', which tends to be an over-simplification used by non-practitioners. Crowley has been accused of many evil things, including recommending blood sacrifice, but since he seemed to take personal pleasure in whatever notoriety was heaped upon him, accurate or not, one can have some sympathy with his major living supporter, Gerald Suster, when he attacks most claims as baseless. Despite Crowley's many writings, it is not an easy path to understand, since his books are frequently deliberately misleading, having hidden meanings, parodies of his enemies and a confusingly obscure literary style.

Chaos Magic

Once again, not all practitioners of Chaos Magic are Pagan, although many are. This is a relatively new field, originating in the 1970s, and has developed within the UK-based Illuminatus Order of Thanateros (IOT) and elsewhere. The two initial major driving forces behind what was initially a small specialist non-hierarchical discussion group were Pete Carroll (1987) and Ray Sherwin (1992), later joined by Phil Hine (1992) and Steve Wilson (1994). Developments include the Pact of IOT (formed by Carroll) and the *Chaos International* magazine.

Chaos magicians start their Magic from a very different premise to most other forms. Whereas most magicians start by building up positive thought forms and correspondences, Chaos magicians try to start from a primal void, where all is confusion and anything is possible. They then adopt a specific paradigm, suitable for their chosen working. Thus they may choose to work within a Celtic mythology one day, Norse another or even Christian or Moslem, depending which they think will be the most suitable and will get the result required. However, many stick to just one particular mythos with which they are familiar. Some have even worked with the 'fictional' mythology of the HP Lovecraft fantasy books.

Chaos magic is specifically results-oriented magic, with an ethos of 'doing whatever works for you', and its use is seen as unethical and disturbing by many other magicians. Central to the practice is the complex mathematical and scientific Chaos Theory as well as Mandelbrot sets, and the automatic writing and sigil creation of Osman Spare.[2] Although it shares a few characteristics with Eclectic Paganism and Witchcraft (the so-called 'pick and mix' approach), it differs in that its practitioners have an ongoing belief in the mythologies they utilise, while *Chaotes* (the practitioners of Chaos Magic) only maintain a belief for the duration of a magical working, and terminate it in favour of others on different occasions, reasoning that all mythologies are personal constructs, and none more valid than the next. This is a very intellectually demanding path to follow, and the only constants are a set of techniques and tools. Joseph Max summarised it:

> Chaos Magic sees nothing but infinite chaos, stochastically[3] dragged into existence by each and every observer according to their predispositions, and by manipulating these predispositions it can be bent in desired directions by a canny intelligence. (Chaosmatrix website)

Voodoo

Voodoo or Vodoun (there are several alternative spellings) is particularly connected with the Anglo-French parts of the Caribbean, especially Haiti, but is also found elsewhere including the UK and USA. It is also closely connected to the Obeah cult, and uses both African Pagan deities and Christian saints within its beliefs. It probably has its ultimate roots in worship of the African snake God Obi.

There is a variant in South America known as Santeria, which combines elements of Yoruba belief with those of the Spanish and Portuguese. In Brazil a variant called Candomble still exists. Many find its darker side of curses, creation of fetish objects, animal sacrifice and zombies either compelling or revolting. Trance work is a principal tool of its priests and priestesses.

Dance and Musical Magic

In Gardnerian Wicca, 'The Witches' Rune' is a combined chant and dance, composed by Gardner and Valiente together. It can be found in *The Witches' Way* (Farrar, 1990). Although dance can be part of a more complex, multidisciplinary approach to magic, it is sometimes used as the magical act itself. Large groups of Pagans will often raise magical energy by forming themselves either into a simple circle or spiral chain forms to dance. (Useful tip: if you are small of stature, do not get attached to the outside part of a spiral dance. It moves much faster than the inside, and you could find difficulty in keeping your feet between two taller people or getting flung out by centrifugal force.) Dance is, of course, a principal part of the religious practices of Native Americans and Australians, but has been almost universal in the past as a spiritual practice. The reason why those Christian Christmas carols have such good tunes is that originally a 'carol' was a Christian circle dance. In recent years there has been an increased interest at some Pagan events in Eastern Temple dance, or to give it its more vulgar name, belly dancing. The women who experience it (and who as Pagans are unashamed in expressing their sexuality) frequently describe it as liberating and empowering, and do not see it as necessarily purely for enjoyment by a male audience. I understand that some are trying to incorporate it into their ritual practices, but it is too early to know whether this will become an established practice as yet.

Current research by Dr Melvyn Willin at Bristol University has already identified several features of music used within rituals. Pre-1950s it was certainly used in some cases to accompany dancing, with whatever musical talent was available providing it, such as a coven member who could play the fiddle. Since then, many different forms of music have been used to enhance rites, including classical and opera, especially those pieces with a mystical or Pagan theme such as *Peer Gynt* (Grieg) or *The Rite of Spring* (Stravinsky).

Many Pagans have contributed to a survey (still being collated) detailing their use of both live and recorded music in ritual. They stress the need for the piece of music being appropriate to the season and ritual, and unobtrusive except for when raising energy or when being played live. More practical uses are to cover external sounds and give direction to the stages of the ritual. New Age music is the most popular, but artistes such as Clannad, Carole Hillyer and Nigel Shaw, Dead Can Dance and Loreena McKennit were all mentioned, alongside Jethro Tull and specifically Pagan artistes Inkubus

Sukkubus, Praying for Rain, Druidspear, Chris Gosselin, Skyclad, Spiral Castle and Legend. Many use folk music by bands such as Steeleye Span, Blowzabella and Fairport Convention. Unsurprisingly the Northern Tradition mentioned Wagner's Ring Cycle and *The Planets Suite* by Holst. It is evident, though, that unaccompanied chanting and playing drums are important to many Pagans in their ceremonies.

Cabbala Magic

It must be said too that the Hebrew Cabbala is the subtlest and richest analysis of the operation of polarity, on all the levels, which is available to Western thinking. (Farrar, 1990)

Although it can be proved that several individuals independently introduced Eastern occult ideas into the UK, I think the most effective of them all was Madame Blavatsky, who formed (with Colonel Olcott) the large and popular Theosophical Society in 1875, which still exists today. An important writer in this field is the Frenchman Eliphas Levi, who has been a major influence on later thinking, especially with his book *A History of Magic* (1913).

Cabbala (to use one of half a dozen spellings) is of Hebrew origin. Although condemned by more Orthodox Jews, it is used by some Jewish scholars today as well as Pagan and non-Pagan magicians alike. It has a very complicated cosmology based around a Tree of Life, through which the adept must progress, with a multitude of angels and elemental beings encountered along the way. There are 22 paths between the ten *Sephiroth* or spheres of influence, which are often equated with the 22 Tarot trumps. One of the techniques of Cabbala is to manipulate certain Hebrew texts into coded grid squares, with numbers being assigned to each letter. Important to this field also are two old texts known as The Greater and Lesser Key of Solomon the King, and astrology and numerology are frequently incorporated into practices.[4] Also much consulted in this field is the book *The Magus* by the Rosicrucian Francis Barrett (1801).

Divination

Trying to predict the future by means of Tarot cards, astrology, the I Ching, runes or scrying, with either a crystal ball or dark mirror, are all forms of magic within themselves, and fulfil a basic human need in an uncertain world. While some churches have warned their congregations not to get involved in such activities, it is surprising how many otherwise devout Christians avail themselves of the services offered. It is a matter of regret by some Pagans that these magical tools are used for profit outside the Pagan context in which they originated. Others believe that a person of skill should be able to earn a modest living from such arts, and that it may help to put people in touch with a side of life to which they are rarely exposed.

As an ex-reader myself, I believe one takes on certain responsibilities when a client pays to have a reading, namely; that the reader should be competent and ethical, and the reading should be honest and make clear the negative aspects as well as the positive. Secondly one should have care for the client in presenting the information so as not to unduly distress them, and should be prepared to listen sympathetically to the stories that they may want to pour out afterwards. Many people seeking readings are in a distressed state, at a crossroads over relationships, jobs or health issues.

Sigil Magic

The skilled graphic artist[5] and policeman's son Austin Osman Spare (1886–1956), who did a lot of experimentation with automatic writing, particularly developed this into a system he called *Zos-Kia Cultus* (Grant, 1975). He developed a method of intuitively drawing symbols representing desired magical effects. These were combined together, simplified and reduced several times so as to obscure original meaning into a distilled magical message (or sigil), which could be activated by burning or burying. This is a gross simplification of the process, which has been much used and adapted, in a number of magical disciplines. Spare was a member of *Argentum Astrum* (AA), a magical order founded by Crowley, and has become a major influence upon Chaos Magic as well as many other fields.

Another form that could be included under this heading is Rune Magic. As well as being used for divination and talismans, runes are also used in Asatru rituals as sigils, chants and postured shapes. Tarot cards also are used outside of their divinatory role for meditations or physical tools within a ritual.

Some General Guidance and Ground Rules

If you choose to follow a Pagan path, sooner or later you may want to conduct a ritual. While this book is not designed to teach magical techniques (see Chapter 17), it is worth mentioning here some general points applicable to most types of magical working. I would emphasise that anything you come up with personally is likely to be at least as valid as anything you can copy from published sources. Books on magical techniques are useful to start you off or to offer tried and tested ideas, but unless you are part of a tradition that insists that things should always be done in the same way, it is generally more satisfying and effective to create your own personalised rituals.

Timing

Some magical systems are very specific as to when things should be done, for example at the waxing, waning or full Moon. If trying to build up a set of sympathetic correspondences, I do believe it is important to 'follow the instructions'. In some other work I think it less relevant or necessary. I cannot imagine an old village Wise Woman or Cunning Man telling a client that nothing could be done for their broken arm until the next full Moon in two weeks' time. Some spells requiring plants state a specific time for them to be gathered. This is generally very important, as plants may need sap rising or to be in their oxygenating phase to be effective. The old herbalists knew this, as do many natural gardeners who sow at specific phases of the Moon.

One should always allow plenty of time for a working. Careful preparation and focus on the intent is as important as the act itself. Try to book a specific time with others or just yourself that you know will be conducive to the right frame of mind. Straight from work, or just after putting the kids to bed or after a heavy meal is not usually advisable, nor is when you are tired or expecting visitors at any moment.

The Place

As a nature religion, we always consider working outside and in contact with natural forces first. A pair of birdwatcher's binoculars is enough to allay the fears and questions of most people that you might meet in the woodland or shore of your choice. Adverse weather should not be a deterrent unless it is dangerous. If you are going to somewhere unfamiliar at night, it is always a good idea to check out the area by daylight first and note any physical obstacles, and to ensure that you can be there legally. Always ensure your personal safety, taking a torch, whistle, compass and mobile phone where appropriate and informing a friend of your whereabouts and expected time of return if you can.

Inevitably, though, there are occasions when you will wish to work indoors. If invited to someone else's home, you should of course respect it, not smoke unless invited to do so and thank them for their invitation. A bottle of wine, cakes or other contribution to the ritual is generally acceptable by most hosts. Some may enjoy flowers, but be careful about this unless you know them, because some Pagans prefer that flowers remain growing in the ground.

If it is your own home, then of course you will want to make any guests welcome. Check out in advance whether they have any special dietary requirements or are averse to any particular practices. For example, are they a diabetic who should not eat sugary foods, or do they have strongly held views about not having metal objects in a circle? Before the ritual starts, you will need to unplug the telephone, put a 'do not disturb' sign by the doorbell, and maybe banish the dog to another room.

The Intent

It is very important to define exactly what you are trying to achieve from a ritual in advance, so that everything can be focused towards its success. It is generally best to define the end objective, but not the means as to how it will be obtained, since magic seems to delight in working in a series of circuitous, seemingly random ways that eventually bring about a conclusion, but not in the way imagined. However, you must have a clear goal, on which everyone working has agreed. Disharmony will spoil the result. You must, of course, consider the ethics of the situation; having an intent of personal gain (other than experience or knowledge) is not generally acceptable within the Pagan world, especially if practical solutions have not been exhausted first. Wishing for an inexhaustible supply of money or sexual partners, or for someone to get ill or die is generally considered unethical!

The Ritual

Some people get very worked up about the word 'ritual'. Yet almost everybody does ritual actions every day, whether it is the order in which we get dressed or the way we make a cup of tea. Ritual is simply a predetermined sequence of actions, designed to achieve a specific outcome in a logical way. Some of the rituals you perform may be laid down in books to a prescribed pattern, in which case you need to think carefully what the desired outcome is to be, and if the ritual is appropriate to your needs. You need to get all the tools, incenses, and so on, together before you start, and consider whether you need to adapt any parts of the ritual. If working with others, have you communicated clearly to them what they are expected to do, and are they in tune with your purpose?

Some Pagans prefer not to work to a set plan, and extemporise their actions and words intuitively as they go along. This is perfectly acceptable, but you do need to have a bit of experience and be confident in what you are doing, otherwise you will be constantly worrying about whether you have done the right thing or missed anything out. Reading from a sheet of paper can hamper the flow and spontaneity of a ritual, so it is as well to rehearse words beforehand (especially any difficult names) and write or print the words large and clearly enough to be read by fire or candlelight. Using clear plastic document wallets is a good idea if you foresee problems with rain or spilt liquids. You could also learn the ritual off by heart, so long as this does not result in losing concentration by worrying whether you can remember the words.

Opening and Closing a Sacred Space

It is usual to create a sacred space to perform your ritual within, whether indoors or out. Even when a well-established one is being used (such as a stone circle), it is usual to perform some form of ritual clearing. Enter the space gently, and ask the spirits of the place for their approval, and explain that you mean them no harm. Wait silently for their reply. Next, the circumference of your space should be defined, by walking round, sprinkling water, wafting incense, sweeping a broom, drawing a circle with a sword or knife, or whatever is preferred. [6] Finally, it is usual to address the four quarters (the cardinal points of the compass), most often starting in the East and ending in the North. People, deities and spirits are welcomed. Some traditions have variations on this pattern, but most reverse the process on closing at the end, so that the direction is clockwise/deosil (in the direction of the sun) for opening, and anti-clockwise/widdershins for closing. Rituals are generally closed by bidding farewell to the spirits and entities who have attended, with a wish that they return to their own realms.

Altered States of Consciousness

It is common practice for people who attempt magic to try to manipulate their mental state in various ways. Before a ritual they may use a technique that constantly refocuses their mind on what they are about to do. An obvious example is fasting. By not eating for many hours beforehand, you may become a little light-headed, and more susceptible to the changes that occur within ritual. Also, because your body will remind you that it wants food, this in turn reminds you that you are going without because of the magic you are about to perform. Thus the ritual becomes the focus for the day, not the meals, work, and so on, that would otherwise have occupied your attention. Other techniques for obtaining altered states are the acts of wearing a special piece of jewellery or garment, going barefoot, abstaining from sex, prolonged meditation, or even the use of drugs or alcohol.

There is a history of magicians using various substances to influence their mental state. Hallucinogenic drugs such as 'magic mushroom' and peyote cactus, alcohol, cannabis or even ordinary tobacco have all found a place within magical practices, especially Shamanism. Personally I would recommend you stay well clear, not just from a legal standpoint but from the view that your body is a temple to the Gods and Goddesses, and should be respected as such. Almost anything achieved by such drugs can be attained by use of more natural means such as dance and chant, fasting, meditation or sleep deprivation.

A Seax Wiccan friend of mine ran courses for people wanting to become Witches. After several weeks of fairly basic level work, they were promised that the next lesson would be about 'altered states of consciousness'. Agog with expectations, they were ushered into a darkened room, and told to wait silently and peacefully. Just as their imaginations had begun to work overtime, the instructor would clash a pair of cymbals very loudly. He would then tell them them, 'There is more than one way to alter states of consciousness!' It was a lesson seldom forgotten.

Just before your ritual, you may want to take a purifying bath, and put on some special robe, clothes or jewellery. This all builds up the focus for the magical act, and sets the situation apart as different and special.

Writing a Ritual

If you are creating a ritual yourself, you need to think of a number of factors.

- Is it suitable for what you want to achieve, and does it relate directly to your core beliefs? Who is the ritual for? Is it for the Gods, the people taking part or for someone else not present? If it is for someone else, do they know what you are doing and do they approve? What are the ethics of the situation?
- Is it suitable for the group of people taking part? If they are a mixed group of Pagans, you may want to avoid using specific God and Goddess names. It may be inappropriate to arrange a dance if any of the participants are disabled, or to make the ritual too deep and complex for a group of beginners. Will the ritual involve as many of them as possible, or will they all stand watching the High Priest and Priestess do everything?
- Is it appropriate to the space, and will it be safe? Is there room enough to dance, and is it safe to wave a sword? Will naked candle flames be too close to people's robes?
- Does it appeal to all the senses? A ritual based upon words only can be dry and boring. The sense of smell can be enlivened with incense, sight by fire, hearing by music, taste by food and drink, and touch by holding hands. Try to avoid having to read the whole thing off a written text. Continually trying to keep your place in your script can distract you. Is it possible

to learn bits off by heart or to allow free expression in some places?

- The best designed ritual in the world will be ineffective if the participants are bored, tired, cold, or distracted by noise, each other, drink and drugs or insects, or if they are nervous of discovery by others. You need to create a safe physical space as well as being focused magically.
- If part of the ritual is intended for frequent use, such as opening a circle, can it be easily duplicated, so that its 'rightness' and sense of ritual is built upon?
- What logistical problems may you face? Will transport be needed, and does the event need to finish before the last bus home? Do you need to produce maps or directions? Do you know the position of North on the ritual site or do you need to take a compass? Does anybody require overnight accommodation or a lift? Will everybody be equipped to walk over rough terrain for a distance? Have you got all the necessary equipment, and the means to transport it? What are the group dynamics of the people you are dealing with, and how will they be likely to respond to instructions?

Earthing

As important as it is to reach a 'higher state' within many rituals, it is equally vital that you return to normality afterwards. This process is usually known as 'earthing', 'centring' or 'grounding'. Essentially this is to return you to the mundane world. While it may seem great to be in tune with the 'other' world, it is not so great if you are trying to drive a car or do something else equally dangerous. A standard part of many ritual celebrations is the 'cakes and ale' (which can just as easily be 'biscuits and wine' or even 'hotdogs and lemonade'). Apart from the globally recognised unifying act of sharing communal food and drink, this serves the very useful purpose of returning you to a normal state. Another way is to touch your fingers to the ground and visualise your magical energies being discharged for the benefit of Mother Earth.

To Know, To Dare, To Will, To Keep Silent. (A Magician's Creed)

Some Final Thoughts

My final advice on this topic is not to fall into the trap of spending so much time theorising about magic and how it works that you never actually get round to attempting any. Just as it is unnecessary to know how a television set works to switch it on, so it is quite possible to work magic without knowing much theory at all. Some people say that magic is far more likely to be effective if you just have confidence that it works. It is worth reflecting on these words by a writer who has been a big influence on my magical thinking, Isaac Bonewits (1989):

> Magic is an art and a science for dealing with particular types of knowledge, the manipulation of which will produce results that will astound and amaze the uninformed. This sounds a great deal like quantum mechanics, cybernetics, and astrophysics, as well as other even more 'occult' sciences. Where is the difference then between magic and science? – Only this: the science and art of magic deals with a body of knowledge that, for one reason or another, has not yet been fully investigated or confirmed by the other arts and sciences.

Things to do

- Using the criteria discussed in this chapter, why not try to make your own simple magical spell? Of course you can try one of the many published spells in other books, but you are far more likely to be successful if you develop your own. 'Simple and direct' is the best approach, focusing on one specific, localised outcome that you are happy with ethically. If you are not sure what method to start with, try writing a spell on a piece of paper, asking the deities for help, chanting it three times and activating it by burning it.

- Make a note of what you did, and what you want to happen, in a special diary, so that you can repeat any successful spells in future.

References

[1] Real name Alphonse-Louis Constant, 1810–75. He also influenced the Theosophists.

[2] Automatic writing consists of inducing a trance state (by whatever means preferred) and allowing the hand to write without any degree of control. Subsequently, messages may be discerned from it. Whether these messages come from the unconscious mind or from an outside spiritual agency is a matter of debate. Sigil writing is performed with a focused magical intention in mind. It may be created in the same way as automatic writing or, alternatively, symbols or phrases are merged together into an unintelligible form, which is subsequently 'sent' by burning it or destroying it in other ways such as burying it.

[3] Stochastic means 'by chance, with no assignable cause'.

[4] Whilst astrology is divination based upon the position of stars and planets within the sky, numerology is concerned with equating letters with numbers (e.g. A = 1, Z = 26) and manipulating them to perceive inner meanings.

[5] He was actually exhibited at the Royal Academy at 19 years old. Although popular within his lifetime, he died in obscurity, probably at least partly because he refused to eschew his working-class roots and pursued his occult interests more than keeping up with connections and trends within his art. He developed his own magical methods which he published in a 1913 book *The Book of Pleasure (Self Love): The Psychology of Ecstasy* and is unusual for his time in that he did not surround himself with large quantities of magical tools and paraphernalia.

[6] It is usually assumed that all Pagans meet in circles. While that is the most frequent format, the traditional Asatru *ve* and the Masonic lodge are rectangular, and there is no reason why any other shape should not be used.

Chapter 15
Where Do We Go From Here?

Divine Earth, mother of men and of the blessed gods,
You nourish all, you give all, you bring all
To fruition, and you destroy all.
(Greek Orphic Hymn – Olsen, 1992)

The Pagan Life

As I have said elsewhere, to be a Pagan (or an adherent of any religion) you have to let the rituals, discussions, books and experiences affect your everyday life, otherwise it is pointless. We should end up living out the words of Sean O'Casey (1926):

> There's no need to bring religion into it. I think we ought to have as great a regard for religion as we can, so as to keep it out of as many things as possible.

Paganism should determine your whole lifestyle – the job you do, the relationships you make, the way you treat others, and your attitude towards the environment. Inevitably this process will bring you into conflict, both with your old ways and habits, and with others around you who may notice changes in you without necessarily knowing the reasons. It can be both a painful and a joyous process, and I have sometimes said that I love my spiritual path, but would not wish it upon my worst enemy!

Choosing a spiritual path presents you with moral dilemmas where there once was no conscious choice. It may make you to want to change career, or even partner. It may cause you to join environ-mental campaigns, stand for election, become a school governor or refuse to buy certain products. Some of this process can be exhilarating and liberating, and can enable you to function to your maximum potential, but as the late playwright Dennis Potter said in a TV interview with Melvyn Bragg in 1994, 'Religion to me has always been the wound, not the bandage.'

How you resolve these dilemmas within your personal life can be quite difficult. It may be that you cannot make the changes you want straight away, which can be frustrating. Changing career, lifestyle or even partner can take a while, and is bound to be a painful process. For example, you might realise that you are working for a company that is at odds with your new beliefs. So you need to decide whether to get another job, or whether it is possible to try to influence the company from within. Some people resolve this dilemma by continuing with their job, while using some of their salary for charitable purposes, or devoting some of their free time to helping the community.

The same principles may apply to your relationships. Is it possi-ble for your partner to become sympathetic to your ideals, or will they always see you in the same stereotypical role, and continue to live in their old non-eco-friendly way? Is it worth staying together for the children's sake? Is it possible to lead a meaningful life in parallel with instead of apart from your partner? You alone can resolve these matters by careful consideration of your personal values and ethics, as well as asking help from your Gods and Goddesses either directly or through divination.

Your new path should have some profound effects on how you live. Some may seem relatively banal, such as wanting to spend a holiday walking across moors to stone circles, but if your partner is not in tune with the same things (and would prefer to be soaking up the sun somewhere) it will inevitably lead to conflict. Can you cope with someone not committed to recycling household waste, or who falls for the traps of the consumer society? What would be the reaction to a man showing a gentler, artistic side and allowing himself to cry? Or to a woman no longer content to take a stereo-typical submissive housewife role, and who in her new-found confidence expecting her mate to share the chores and free her to pursue interests of her own? It is possible for a mixed belief couple to resolve such issues successfully, and thought should be given as to how this can be achieved harmoniously.

Coming out of the Broom Closet

Although you have a right to hold and proclaim your spiritual views, whether to 'come out' publicly as a Pagan is a difficult choice. It is much easier now than a few years ago. More people are aware of us and have become tolerant of different religions. Although one can adopt the idea that 'prejudice is their problem, not mine', for some people in sensitive jobs or living in shared accommodation it can be very difficult, despite our anti-discrimination legislation. For this reason one must always be careful of not accidentally 'outing' other Pagans you meet against their wishes. Personally I have never had a problem with being publicly known as a Pagan, but I know others that have.

It is important to think how your declaration will affect others. Is it really worth upsetting an aged, devoutly Christian relative for the sake of it? In any case, the question should rarely arise. Pagans have no need to proselytise, or use their beliefs as a means to deliberately shock or offend people. I think it is offensive for Pagans to force their views and persuasion onto every passing stranger. We do, after all, find it offensive to be preached at by people of other religions.

Dealing with Evangelism

Whilst most Pagans would agree to the need to be tolerant to other religions, regarding them as being different paths – of no lesser or greater importance – to the same essential truths, many suffer from that respect not being reciprocated. Consequently, some Pagans may require some defence against those fundamentalists of other religions who are determined to impress on you how theirs is the only true and unquestionable path. Whilst a simple 'no' or 'not interested' are the simplest ways of dealing with such people, some fanatics may not accept this answer. Understandably, some Pagans may find this process challenging and often feel unable to deal with it adequately.

Having dealt with the enquiries of many newbie Pagans over the years, a very frequent request is how to deal with people who assume that they are Christian, or try to evangelise them into becoming one. Inevitably you will at sometime be confronted by this problem, generally via doorstep evangelists, but possibly through a work colleague, friend or relation expecting you to share their views or to join in with their religious activities. Think in advance what response may be appropriate, lest you be caught unawares.

To someone new to Paganism, being confronted in this way can be very daunting, but remember you are under no obligation to discuss your spirituality with relations, employers or officials, let alone anyone knocking on your door without an invitation. Saying 'no thank you' is certainly the easiest way of dealing with the nuisance, but I think the sheer arrogance of people wanting to force their religious opinions onto others is some justification for more confident Pagans to take them on at their own game. I would stress that 'I'm not prepared to discuss my private spirituality with you' is the simplest way of dealing with the matter, but nevertheless I offer below some advice for the minority who persist in carrying on regardless. It also might be of use to those who are feeling guilty about rejecting the faith that they have been brought up in. We as Pagans should be honest enough to admit some of the inconsistencies within our own beliefs,[1] and in doing so realise that this applies to other people, not because their path is unwholesome as such, but because extremism and dogma can be.

I remember the first time I invited two Jehovah's Witnesses into my house, on the understanding that I would listen to them for ten minutes then they would listen to me for ten minutes in return. My lodger at the time cringed in the kitchen and accused me afterwards of 'playing with them'. Needless to say, neither they nor their ilk ever bothered me again, despite calling on all my neighbours!

I am not anti-Christian (I was one myself until about 14 years old), but I think it's worth being aware the Bible upon which they rely as a factual source is very inconsistent. For example, the 'Feeding of the 5,000' is done with a different number of loaves and fishes, depending on which gospel you read. And what about Adam, who was told by God that he was to die the same day he ate the forbidden fruit (Genesis 2:17)? Elsewhere in Genesis it says he lived until he was 930 years old! Talking of Genesis, it is always worth pointing out that the 'Elohim' credited with creating humanity (Genesis 1:28) is in fact a Hebrew plural word for Gods, including both male and female. Moreover, if you examine Genesis carefully you will find that it refers to humans outside the Garden of Eden who do not follow Yahweh, which is probably why Yahweh is referred to as a 'jealous God'.

If you want to try a more direct approach with doorstep evangelists, and you are feeling hard up, why not ask them for their wallet? All you need to quote is Luke 6:30: 'Give to everyone that asketh thee, and from him that taketh away thy goods ask them not again.' Similarly, if the evangelist is against drinking, why not quote 'take a little wine for thy stomach's sake'. I was recently delighted to relocate the reference I once found that said that no man shall approach the altar of the Lord with imperfect vision (Leviticus 21:18), which implies that we can dismiss any evangelists with spectacles or contact glasses as not being proper Christians! Seriously though, there are some excellent theological studies exposing the inconsistencies of the Bible. As suggested above, they can be quite entertaining, particularly when used in dialogue with those people who believe that the Bible is completely factually true. As for that much quoted 'Thou shalt not suffer a witch to live', in the original language the text read 'poisoner' rather than 'witch'. King James, who had the Bible translated into English, was very anti-witchcraft and so lumped witches and poisoners together. For the more mischievous-minded, there are also some amusing Web sites (see Chapter 17), containing some real biblical gems for quoting to unwelcome evangelists.

Dealing with the Media

Most Pagans avoid talking to reporters, and that is understandable. However, if you become a public figure in the Pagan world, there is always the possibility that you may be asked to speak to the press. You may even want to seek them out if you are publicising a conference or other event. Media training is a complex subject, and advice is available from organisations such as the Pagan Federation.

Think about what you are prepared to say or do beforehand, and do not go beyond that limit. If they demand more, refuse to co-operate. Remember, in most cases they need you more than you need them.

Networking

It is perfectly possible to be an isolated individual Pagan, but we are essentially social animals who benefit from the support of a group environment. It is therefore natural that you might want to make contact with other like-minded individuals, with a view to working together. This might be at a moot, a conference, or within an organisation, coven or hearth. Recommended organisations to contact are listed in Chapter 17. They will often be very useful in helping you make more local contacts. The organisations, books and Web sites I am recommending in this book are all ones in which I have confidence.

However, organisations are unable to personally verify the honesty and integrity of every individual contact. You have to take personal responsibility for whoever you choose to meet with. As in any group, within Paganism there is the occasional individual who is less scrupulous, but I have always found the majority of Pagans to be decent, honest and ethical people. However, it is as well to be aware that such characters exist (as they do in almost every religion), particularly if you are just starting to explore Paganism and are making contacts. They tend to target newcomers as a source of achieving power, or financial or sexual favours. The general Pagan community is aware of most of these charlatans, and will be keen to advise whom to watch out for.

It is best to be on your guard if you encounter a Pagan with an important-sounding title, who seems really keen to 'convert' you or have you join their group (often promising that great secrets will be revealed when you do). Paganism in its modern sense is unique as a religion in that it is non-proselytising. It is against most Pagans' ethics to try to coerce someone into joining a religious path that is often hard, and which might be totally unsuitable for the individual concerned. We are generally willing to answer questions, write, teach, broadcast or lecture, but only to those who want to find out more.[2] The general feeling is that 'my religion may be absolutely ideal for me personally, but because it is so individual it may not be suitable for anyone else at all.'

Furthermore, there are no particularly important secrets left for anyone to pass on, other than the identity of other Pagans. Fifty years ago, the wording of rituals, spells, and so on, was a closely-guarded secret. Nowadays most have been published several times for all to read, and the only secret rituals are those made up by someone yesterday. If somebody had an enormously powerful, valuable secret, why would want to tell it to a completely inexperienced, unknown beginner anyway? A final tell-tale sign of many charlatans is the grandiose titles they award themselves. Ask yourself why anyone should want to be known as anything as inflated as 'The Most High, Grand Purple Octopus, Guardian of the Ninth Crystal Abyss' and you will see what I mean. Although there are some specific titles given to certain experienced Pagans, the rest of the Pagan world usually attaches very little value to them, and I include my own titles in that. Pagans tend to be keen on pricking pomposity.

Of course, it is natural that like-minded people should want to get together, particularly when they feel they are in a religious minority.[3] The use of moots, conferences and special interest groups, as well as some useful Web sites, is a very positive development of modern Paganism. However, I would urge caution when meeting people for the first time. Meet in a neutral place and do not give your address to anyone you are unsure of. Let someone else know where you are going if you can, or arrange for a friend to phone you after half an hour. Nobody who is open and honest will object to this. Do not give away personal details to others on the Web without considering it carefully. It is also considered good etiquette not to reveal others' names, addresses, e-mail, etc., without their permission.

Incidentally, you will find that many Pagan individuals and organisations in the UK have an address of BM: (name), London, WC1N 3XX. It is not that they all live in some multi-storey Pagan office block, but that British Monomark is the sole licensed national mail forwarding service. As well as allowing organisers to keep their own address private, it allows organisations to redirect mail easily when the staff change.

Moots

Moots are social gatherings of Pagans of various paths from a specific geographic area. They take place mainly in pubs, but also in individual houses or even coffee shops. They can vary in size and nature enormously. In my own mainly rural area of East Anglia there are around 17, compared with none only ten years ago. Some comprise just half a dozen members, while some may attract 100 to 150 people. Some merely have a social discussion, while others feature a planned programme of lectures, mini-talks, open rituals, visits and environmental clean-up campaigns and other projects. Some (particularly those in people's houses) are by invitation only, and may make a small charge for refreshments. Others may charge for visiting speakers, but otherwise cost no more than buying a drink at the bar. They are a very good way to meet other Pagans and compare ideas and paths and swap information. It also allows you meet people socially before committing yourself to joining a group or coven, and to discuss things openly without being thought 'weird'.

Conferences

The growth in Pagan conferences in the last five years has been phenomenal. As well as several national events in the UK attracting over 1,000 people each, a whole network of more than 20 annual regional conferences has developed, catering for 100 to 200 people. You can expect to find speakers on a variety of topics, debate on hot issues, join a ritual (often the first opportunity for many new Pagans to participate in one), and enjoy music, dance, socialising, eating and drinking.

As a frequent lecturer and attendee, I never fail to be impressed with the creativity, joyous good feeling and diversity of such events, whether large or small. They have become a real focus and rallying point for many, and some have developed into annual camping events, allowing people to renew old acquaintances. It has been my experience that the newcomer is made very welcome at these events, and the one practical precaution I would advise is to plan your leaving time early. It will take half an hour to hug everybody goodbye!

The Pagan Community

When Paganism formed the dominant group of world religions, it was responsible for great art, poetry, architecture, mathematics, democracy and legal procedure. It is therefore hardly surprising that as you explore the Pagan community you will find a great subculture of Pagan music, books, fashion, magazines, poetry, TV programmes, films and art. There are more intangible facets to Pagan lifestyle as well, such as a wickedly ironic, earthy humour, wearing lots of jewellery and spending more on books and computers than the national average!

Because of our special interest in history, many Pagans become very involved with historical societies or re-enactment groups. Many are keen to find out more about the religious practices and general culture of their ancestors, so become very interested in history itself. This may in part be put down to our questioning of historical sources, which were censored or re-written, or which were biased by the beliefs of their authors.

Many Pagans become exponents of fantasy art, literature and role-playing games. With no moral imperative to 'act like grown-ups', you are free to be as playful as a child, and experience childlike excitement and wonder without guilt. A few years ago I attended a ritual on a hilltop. It was a simple affair, with a meditation and some chanting and singing. When we finished, it was time to walk back down the hill. One chap decided to roll down it instead, and was soon copied by most of the rest of us, laughing as we tumbled over and over to the bottom. This caused amusement and bewilderment to some hikers coming up the other way. Yes, we experienced the Earth in a new way that day (and had the bruises to prove it), but that was not the point. We had spontaneously allowed ourselves to play in an unselfconscious way, with no worry about being thought silly or undignified.

Our religion has materialized itself in the fact, in the supposed fact; it has attached its emotions to the fact, and now the fact is failing it. But for poetry the idea is everything; the rest is a world of illusion, of divine illusion. Poetry attaches its emotion to the idea; the idea is the fact. The strongest part of our religion today is its unconscious poetry. (Matthew Arnold, 1888)

As Wallace Stevens (1957) puts it, 'The poet is the priest of the invisible.' It is a very relevant fact that many mythologies and Pagan paths place great importance on the role of the poet (such as the Pagan Matthew Arnold), who can often distil a wealth of ideas and experience into a few thought-provoking words. Many Pagans try to encapsulate their religious feelings in poetry, which has the advantage of conveying profound ideas without necessarily sounding pompous. Whether you think you are very 'good' at poetry or not, I would recommend that you try it. Similarly, expressing yourself in art or craftwork can be a great route to spiritual development and enlightenment.

> Art and Religion then are two roads by which men escape from circum-stance to ecstasy. Between aesthetic and religious rapture there is a family alliance. Art and Religion are means to similar states of mind. (Clive Bell, 1914)

Forming a Pagan Group

Many may find the ideal group, coven or hearth to join, but not everybody is so lucky. Possibly your local covens have closed themselves to new members, or perhaps there is not a group of your particular orientation within reach, or perhaps you simply do not like the people in the one that is. If you want to celebrate with others, you may have to form a working group yourself (unless your chosen path is one in which you feel you need to be initiated by another).

Forming your own group is not always as daunting as it seems. For a start, nobody can forbid you to do so – Paganism is an open group of religions. You do not have to be an expert. I have seen several successful groups where none of the original founders knew much. They were honest about this, and learnt together. If you a drawn to one particular path, it is possible that a relevant specialist organisation can help set you up a group and give you contacts and support, sending publicity to like-minded individuals, and helping with training.

Starting a group is a responsibility, however. Think carefully about what the focus is to be, how you will operate and what ground rules you will set before advertising yourselves in Pagan magazines, shop notice boards and the like. You should also try to be choosy about who you admit, rather than allow everyone in and then realise you are stuck with people you do not feel comfortable working with. You are likely to end up as pseudo-parent, counsellor and social organiser, as well as priest/priestess, so set some boundaries initially as to when and how people can contact you, confidentiality, financial arrangements, expected behaviour, and so on. It is much better that people know what to expect than have acrimonious disputes later.

Working Solo

If you live in a remote area, or have such a specialised path that very few other people are interested in it, you may have to work solo. Some people prefer this anyway, rather than fitting in with other people and making compromises, while others work solo while they are trying to find or form a group. Although I work with two ritual groups, I still enjoy going off alone once in a while. There are certainly advantages as well as disadvantages. It can be lonely, but it can also be very satisfying to create one's own, very personalised rituals.

If you still crave some contact with other Pagans, make use of the Internet, moots and conferences, as well as specialist organisations and magazines to stimulate your interest and give you fresh ideas. The popularity and availability of the World Wide Web has revolutionised the way that many Pagans operate. In my experience, more Pagans work professionally in information technology than the average for any other grouping within society, which is at odds with the image some Pagans have as living in the past. I think its 'magic' and potential for creativity appeal to Pagans. Even more Pagans use the Web from home. Pagans have been meeting in chat rooms and e-groups for at least ten years to discuss ideas and to perform rituals. I know of rituals where a magic circle was drawn in cyberspace across the whole of the USA. Somebody on the Canadian border invoked the elements of the North, with people on the east coast, west coast and in the south carrying out a similar process for their respective cardinal points. People co-operating en masse online can frequently produce a truly gigantic ritual without ever meeting face-to-face.

There are some impressive Web sites created by Pagans around the world on just about every esoteric topic you can think of. These, and their associated chat rooms and restricted e-groups, are a boon to the isolated Pagan who has little opportunity for contact with others. Inevitably, not everything that comes out of Web sites is accurate, but the same could be said about information in books and magazines.

Things to do

- If you have decided to be a Pagan, consider whether you should be open about your beliefs or not. If you feel life would be simpler and it would not threaten family and work relationships to 'come out', plan how you would like to do it in a controlled way.

- If you have not done so before, consider the possibility of contacting and interacting with some fellow Pagans. You could go to a moot or conference, or join a specialist organisation or local group. It is a big step, but for most people it proves very satisfying and rewarding.

References

[1] For example, believing in not harming any one, yet harming ourselves with tobacco, alcohol, junk food, etc.

[2] This does have the side-effect of making us quite difficult to find, since we do not advertise ourselves or even have public buildings people can go to. Being a nature religion we tend to practise in the open air in woods and stone circles and on beaches, although some use their own garden or a space especially set aside in their home.

[3] In the UK it is always assumed that Christians are the religious majority. I would challenge this, since only a maximum of 10 per cent of the UK population go to any sort of church on a regular basis. (I understand the figure is nearer 35 per cent in the USA.)

Chapter 16
The Future of Paganism

Everywhere, ordinary people are searching for some-thing to fill a gap in their lives, and for many the established religions simply don't do the trick anymore.
(Mark Chadbourn, *The Times*, 27 January, 2001)

The Future of Spirituality

The established Church of England is in disarray. Its special envoy, the ex-Beirut hostage Terry Waite, is quoted in *The Times* (20 January, 2001) as saying, 'I think the Church of England is finished, dead. I think it will be disestablished and probably join with the free Churches and the Methodists.' While some may derive a certain amount of glee from that statement (whether it proves true or not), it should give the Pagan community cause for concern.

We tend to welcome anybody who appears to have a genuine interest in our beliefs, and the majority of UK Pagans (including myself) were originally brought up as Christians to a greater or less-er extent. If only a fraction of former members of that Church became disenchanted, and sought new spiritual meaning within our ranks, among others, our community could be swamped. Worse still, if that group became a majority, and brought ideas of orthodoxy and hierarchy with them, the face of Paganism would be altered for ever, and return to a form more akin to the state-governed model of Ancient Rome. It is not that we should reject anybody from enjoying our spiritual path, but that we should be cautious of the influences that they may innocently bring with them.

We comprise a collection of religious paths without any particular dogma or hierarchy prescribing how we should interpret our Pagan beliefs. When the lone individual enters our community (which tends to grow slowly and organically), they tend to pick up on the cues given by it, and re-examine their previously held ideas. However, if a large contingent of people with the same basic ideas entered the community together, they might not make the changes in attitude necessary for them to live a free-form Pagan existence. For example, they might look for some authoritative leader, rather than decide intuitively what was right for them, thus losing the essential element of finding one's own personal path. We should welcome new Pagans, but on our terms rather than theirs.

It is important to appreciate that our form of religious expression is just not suitable for many people. I do not think that this elitist, but merely realistic. A large proportion of any population is conditioned (often through no fault of their own) to take the line of least resistance, not to ask too many questions and to consume what others prepare for them, whether that be news, food, history, shopping or religious beliefs. It is possible for some to change and adapt to more challenging ways of living, but such a path would not be enjoyed by many. I think we do them a disservice if we encourage a section of society to be dissatisfied with their lot, yet not provide them with a suitable alternative, which they can appreciate. This idea is just one of the driving forces behind our determination as a community not to try to convert people to our way of thinking.

I have always wanted Church and State to be separate, since like many I object to part of the UK House of Lords being filled with unelected Christian bishops who govern my life. Having said that, the experience of ex-Eastern Bloc countries being suddenly given an even playing field for religious activity has been that major, well-funded evangelism has taken place on an unprecedented scale, swamping all competition. Inevitably though, even without such a major influx, the Pagan population around the world continues to grow organically and to thrive, as people discover the effects wrought on our world by those who do not have its best interests at heart.

Interfaith and Intrafaith

There can be no ongoing human society without a world ethic for the nations.
There can be no peace among the nations without peace among the religions.
There can be no peace among the religions without dialogue among the religions.
(Hans Kung – www.interfaith.org)

We need to endeavour to understand the religious thoughts of others without committing ourselves to being converted to them. There is an interfaith network in its infancy, where liberal-minded members of many faiths get together to explore similarities and differences. The overriding rule within such discussions is to respect another's right to a different opinion to one's own. Some Pagans have an aversion to interfaith talk, believing it to be the 'enemy' wanting to find out information to use against us. Although there might be a few vociferous fundamentalists of various religions who would like to do just that, they tend not to join interfaith groups, or be welcomed into them. However, the problem exists that although open-minded liberal members of various religions can meet peace-fully and beneficially together, unless they are able to persuade their respective religious communities of the benefit of dialogue and take meaningful messages back to them, then the effort will be wasted. This applies to Pagans as much as any other religious grouping, and I think we must face the fact that we can have fundamentalists in our midst as well.

It is perfectly possible for open-minded Moslem, Sikh, Baha'i, Jewish, Hindu, Christian, Buddhist and Pagan people to meet together agreeably, and to tell each other about their beliefs without trying to say that their way is the best, or only, path. They will find they share some universal beliefs regarding being good to each other, the importance of the family, and so on, as well as coming to an understanding of how different paths and cultures have arrived at different opinions on some subjects. The problem comes when they return to their own religious groups. Some may be interested to find out what has been learnt about other people and their beliefs, but there will often be many others who are unwilling to listen, whether through prejudice or ignorance, or even because they feel their own faith may be at risk if they hear contradictory ideas. This is not to say that interfaith cannot work, because it does, and I think it will become increasingly successful due to the greater tolerance expected within a multi-cultural society. Much of its value is built on personal relationships between individuals. It is hard to be prejudiced against a person's beliefs when you have spent the afternoon with them drinking tea and comparing photos of your grandchildren.

Some very good practical things have come out of interfaith. In my old home town of Ipswich, the Suffolk Inter Faith Resource (SIFRe) has jointly constructed a peace garden, and organised lectures, visits to different places of worship and multifaith celebrations in the town, as well as producing two group publications (Capey, 1993 and 1995). When the Sikh temple was flooded just before a major festival, volunteers from various other religions within SIFRe rallied round to help them out in various ways. The local Pagans organised a marquee for them. On such actions lasting friendships are made, and we were all invited to join in their celebration.

The same arguments apply internally to the Pagan community, in the area of intrafaith – dialogue between various Pagan persuasions. Until we can learn to accept the differences between the various Pagan paths, we shall remain unable to relate successfully to the wider spiritual world. All religious groupings are subject to sub-division, usually a result of dissidents breaking away from the main force. This is very evident in the fragmentation of Christianity and Islam, where each component part acknowledges a particular divinity, but perceives an independent way of actualising it. So it is within Paganism, with the further complication that there is a bewildering multiplicity of deities. Most paths share similar principles and ideas, but use different names. We should celebrate our right to be different and free-thinking, rather than clinging on to the petty personal squabbles that led to division in the first place.

Organisations

The days of ramshackle inefficient Pagan organisations uniting a small group of dedicated people is nearly past. With the growth of the Pagan community in general, its organisations have become larger and more visible. With that comes members' expectations that a magazine will arrive on time, and will be of reasonable quality, that letters will be answered promptly, that events will happen as publicised. The growth in membership may include people who are not as heavily involved or committed as the original band of activists, and they may want to see concrete results such as a magazine or conference for their money, rather than the other important activities the organisation is involved in. That is all very well if the organisation has a paid staff, proper offices and a membership willing to give a realistic subscription to pay for it all. In reality, that situation is a long way off, but inevitably it means that the hard-working volunteers who run such organisations burn out quickly, and become disillusioned trying to run things on a kitchen table in their spare time between job and family commitments. They can try to organise themselves more efficiently and act more professionally, or even sub-contract work out, but most struggle under the weight of working for organisations too small to have paid help but too big to do without it. When they do get better organised, they may be accused of being too remote from the grass roots, and on some sort of ego trip. When they have the temerity to suggest that Pagans should do things to an agreed timetable, they may be accused of being dictators!

There are basically two solutions. We could lower our expectations, and keep a cosy small-team atmosphere, or help spread the load by offering our own time, talents and/or money. Unfortunately, few see it that way; as in most human activity, there are the 'doers' and the 'watchers'. You have to decide which you are to be.

Being active in the Pagan community does not necessarily mean taking on a prominent, high-pressure position. Is there a moot in your area? If you are a 'doer', why not start one? Just find a suitable place and time and advertise it – it is as simple as that! You do not need great experience or knowledge, just a desire to make things happen. You can apply the same principles to conferences, magazines, Web sites, and so on. There will generally be a more experienced individual from an adjacent area only too willing to give advice.

The future of Paganism is dependent on the quality as well as quantity of the people involved in it. As we strive towards a higher sensitivity and awareness of the natural world and ourselves, we are capable of changing the world to be a better place. The battle might seem hopeless at times, and we may find ourselves adopting unusual tactics and allies, but each person doing their best in whichever part of the battlefield they find themselves will win most battles.

Expectations

As Pagans become more organised, network better and consequently become more vocal, they are more certain to be noticed. The results of this could be positive or negative. On the positive side, their demands for an environmentally friendly government, and religious tolerance and parity are less easy to ignore. Where once Pagans could be marginalised as a secretive cult of old hippies, it is less easy to dismiss educated, well-presented professional people, confident in manipulating the media and unafraid of being personally identified. This is already happening, with Pagan organisations able to call upon the skills of media, medical, social work and legal professionals committed to working for their beliefs. They are also able to count on the support, or at least neutrality, of many leading newspapers, and television and radio producers who have been successfully educated over the last decade through constant and costly media operations. Many Pagans have agreed to do interviews for the first time, and dispense with anonymity in taking part in serious factual documentaries and articles. From a position of having to combat wildly inaccurate, lurid tales of devil worshipping, baby eating and virgin sacrificing, we are most likely nowadays to be asked to offer the Pagan perspective on a number of current issues, without the need to defend ourselves so much. Inevitably there is the occasional tacky tabloid piece, but they are as likely to do 'naughty vicar' stories as to bother us much or be believed by the general public.

However, this process of professionalism may well alienate some other existing Pagans, who prefer to remain secretive (or glory in being free, rebellious spirits) and who do not wish others to speak on their behalf, even though they are unwilling to speak up for themselves. Occasionally, I even meet Pagans who seem to want to be oppressed, either actually or within their own imagination, as if uniting against the anonymous and nebulous 'them' would somehow unite 'us'. I remember a controversy a few years ago when a few influential Pagans began discussing the future possible need for a trained, ordained reliable priest/priestess elite. Although the idea was dismissed by most, it did have the value of drawing out the usually more reticent members of our community, who railed against the thought of any form of dogma corrupting the free flow of Pagan ideas and ideals, and defining who was a Pagan and who not.

Unfortunately, as Paganism becomes more evident as a viable force, it is inevitable that those who oppose it will orchestrate a backlash. Fundamentalists of other religions are sure to make attacks, whether physical or by propaganda. On both sides of the Atlantic there have been substantial campaigns to shun Hallowe'en and remove books (such as the popular *Harry Potter* stories) with a magical element in them from schools. In the past, occult shops have been firebombed and individuals threatened. The satanic ritual abuse scare was spread throughout Britain until the UK Government, in the shape of the 'La Fontaine' Report (1994), decided that police and social services had been wilfully misled into removing children from parents by an extremist evangelist group. Social workers had broken their own rules and further complicated matters by conducting prolonged, leading-question interviews with minors. In a key conclusion regarding allegations of satanic abuse, the Report stated: 'Their defining characteristic is that sexual and physical abuse of children is part of rites directed to a magical or religious objective. There is no evidence that these have taken place in any of the 84 cases studied.' In the USA the FBI met a similar conclusion after an extensive two-year operation. In over 200 cases investigated alleging ritual murder, not a single charge was brought or a corpse found. Of course, this did not prevent some extreme anxiety being felt in the Pagan community during the investigations. We therefore have to remain vigilant against the threats of extremists, and continue to support financially or physically the efforts of individuals and organisations who work in our defence. In a 1985 survey of 'What is the most important thing you want to tell the public about Paganism and the Craft?', more than half the responses were summarised by Adler (1986) as:

> We are not evil. We do not worship the Devil. We don't harm or seduce people. We are not dangerous. We are ordinary people like you. We have families, jobs, hopes and dreams. We are not a cult. We are not weird. This religion is not a joke. We are not what you think we are from looking at TV. We are real. We laugh, we cry. We are serious. We have a sense of humour. You don't have to be afraid of us. We don't want to convert you. And please don't try to convert us. Just give us the same right we give you – to live in peace. We are much more similar to you than you think.

It is interesting that so many of those statements were apologist defences against negative images, rather than positive statements such as 'we love nature' or 'the Goddess is liberating' that we might have expected. The attitudes were gathered mainly from American Pagans in 1985. I believe that attitudes have become a lot more positive or even defiant since then, with the braver elements (possibly encouraged by anti-discriminatory legislation in other areas) saying, 'I'm not prepared to put up with prejudice any longer – we are the good guys.'

The Greying of Paganism

Many people who first became involved in Paganism and Witchcraft during the late 1950s to early 1960s are now of pensionable age. Over the last few years we have lost such important figures as Doreen Valiente, Cecil Williamson, Stewart Farrar and many others. People who came into Paganism slightly later now have children grown to adulthood and even grandchildren. This will all have an important impact on the way the movement develops.

There is an inherent respect for the Elders within most forms of Paganism, and we should benefit from the advice our seniors can give us based upon their experience. Indeed, it is often seen as something fairly unique in the Western world to appreciate the older generation. It is also important, however, that those in senior positions allow the traditions to progress, so that younger adherents can develop the path without being for ever artificially frozen in the thinking of an earlier time. A religious path is useless if it cannot relate to the lives of people, as they are now. Younger Pagans must also think carefully when organising events. Is access suitable for those of a less nimble body? Is the content of the event likely to appeal to older, experienced Pagans?

Young Pagans

At the other end of the scale, organisers of conferences need to decide whether there will be activities suitable for youngsters, or whether a crèche will be available. Children who are second- or even third-generation Pagans are becoming more common. There has been heated debate as to whether children should be brought up as Pagans, or left until they are older to explore and make up their own minds. The difficulty occurs because they will be subjected to other religious pressures as they grow up. How can they make a balanced decision later if they have not been supplied with an equal amount of facts about Paganism? As a Pagan parent, you might have to decide whether your child should attend religious education classes or school assemblies. Only you can decide what is the best option for your particular situation. Do you tell them about your beliefs at all? If they pass this on to their friends, will they become ostracised, bullied or discriminated against? Or is theirs the better sort of school where you can openly explain your concerns and feelings with a teacher?

Of course it is not just our own children we have to deal with. Many children from differing religious backgrounds may approach our Pagan organisations for advice. Single TV programmes or articles in UK teenage magazines (such as *Bliss*) have each generated over 1,000 letters from young would-be witches. Admittedly some were probably simply attracted by the notion of casting spells, but a large proportion (undoubtedly frequently driven by environmental concerns) were serious inquirers.

It has been the practice in the past for many Pagan organisations (afraid of being seen as proselytising or even corrupting) to refuse to deal with children under 18. Some organisations are now modifying this practice to work with younger people with parental consent.

We cannot continue to be forced to say to our children, 'This is beautiful, sacred and meaningful – but don't tell anyone about it!' (Starhawk, 1979)

The Media

The media, for good or bad, inevitably drives much of the interest in Paganism, magic and the occult. The series of *Harry Potter* books by JK Rowling has been the publishing phenomenon of the decade, and other books and television programmes with magical or supernatural themes (such as *Buffy the Vampire Slayer* or *Sabrina the Teenage Witch*) have also caught the general public's imagination. There is much that can be learnt about the nature of the Pagan world and magic in the successful and hilarious *Discworld* novels of Terry Pratchett. Inevitably, it only takes one person to want ban a book or film (such as *The Craft*, or *The Blair Witch Project*), for it to become popular.

One of the quirks of this market is that adults seize upon the best juvenile material too, happy to indulge in some escapist fantasy adventure and humour. If you look at the list of most popular books for children to read (and parents to borrow), you will find a high proportion have a magical content, such as CS Lewis's 'Chronicles of Narnia' (even though this was a Christian allegory), JRR Tolkien's *The Lord of the Rings* or the books of Roald Dahl. In addition, the adult fantasy 'sword and sorcery' genre of fiction is still immensely popular and widely read by people who have no other direct contact with the esoteric world. Inevitably, the popularity of all the forms mentioned has brought a type of acceptance or normalisation of ideas that would not have seen wide circulation a few decades ago. In theory this should make people more tolerant of Paganism, but it inevitably backfires from time to time when a popular film, programme or newspaper publishes inaccurate or highly biased material. That is why it is so important for Pagans individually and collectively to challenge inaccurate portrayals, and make sure the media has access to reliable material.

Some Conclusions

It seems as though Paganism will continue to thrive and grow into the foreseeable future. An increasing percentage of that growth will be of intelligent, articulate professionals. Being gradual, such growth will be sustainable, but will inevitably bring with it organisational problems as well as the pleasures of being large enough to be effective. (Already we are seeing an increasing trend in Pagan groups being big enough to buy woodland to preserve for their own use.) There will inevitably be further sub-divisions, new trends and specialisations developing within Pagan organisations. Although occasionally traumatic for individuals at the time, in the light of past experience this is usually seen as healthy development by an individualistic, unfettered movement, rather than the destructive schisms experienced in more authoritarian religions.

Anti-discriminatory legislation will take some time to take effect, but should eventually be beneficial to Pagans. Many test cases will be needed to clarify its details, and to act as a deterrent to those reluctant to act within its precepts. If you can remember how long anti-racist or anti-sexist laws have been in place (and how long it took them to take effect), then you can see that the road to enforced religious equality will be a long one, marked by the sacrifices of those who refuse to accept prejudice. There will always those who celebrate their spirituality in a quiet, private and non-confrontational way, but there are a growing number who choose to be more public. There are many more quite militant Pagans now, who are no longer prepared to stay in the shadows or put up with discrimination of any kind, for any longer. The health of Paganism will always depend on those prepared to be proactive, the 'doers' rather than the 'watchers', who must be content with the pace and nature of change provided by others or else become 'doers' themselves, as spiritual warriors. Brian Bates (1983) sums it up well:

> The greatest fighters live as an arrow, not a target. The arrow speeds through space cleanly, swiftly, directly; alive and moving, it has direction and an end point, but in between it soars. The target merely stays still, waiting for something to happen.

Not only must you decide which Pagan path to tread; it is important to decide whether you intend to be an arrow or a target. We need targets for stability and continuity, but we also need our arrows to innovate, adapt, develop and organise.

Having no overall, hierarchical leadership means that changes only happen over a gradual period by a popular change in the consensus of general opinion. This may mean that as a collective, we may take time to respond to new developments, but it also means that individuals and small groups are free to take their own localised decisions, and not feel disenfranchised by a remote leadership making decisions with which they disagree.

The lack of clear leadership and environmental responsibility in the larger world religions has not reflected the growing awareness of young people who are taught to respect nature and question authority. Inevitably they will feel more at home within spiritual paths that reflect their own values. Their influx should keep our theology and actions relevant to today's world whilst having a basis in ancient values. With the exception of Hinduism, I do not foresee a time when Paganism regains a position of being a world religion with an enormous number of followers. Our path is too hard and demanding for the casual follower. It does not suit those who want everything to be carefully thought out on their behalf, and presented in easily digestible chunks. It is still going to be the province of independent, intelligent free-thinkers, with a love of the natural world and a self-motivated desire for spiritual and personal growth.

In writing this book, I have not sought to convert anyone to Paganism. If it has helped to clarify what Paganism is, and has led you to make personal decisions about your future spiritual path (Pagan or not), I wish you joy on your individual journey.

> No one can make us Pagans. We are Pagans if our beliefs match those of Pagan thought and we consider ourselves to be so. Particular Pagan paths may have entry through a dedication ceremony, initiation or adoption into a family or clan; but these offer gateways into their own paths only. People can be Pagans without any of these ceremonies. Paganism teaches that many answers to the problems of the present lie in the forgotten wisdom of the past; but unlike Western religions, Paganism does not claim to possess a monopoly on religious truth. (Crowley, 1995)

Things to do

- Thank you for reading this book. I hope it will be the beginning of an interesting journey for you. Think about the main ideas you have read about and also consider the things that you have disagreed with. I shall be disappointed if you have agreed with everything I have said!

- If you have decided upon a specific Pagan path, check out the recommended books, Web sites, references and organisations in Chapter 17. They should also be a good resource for anyone wishing to find out more about a specific topic.

- Where you have skimmed over footnotes, go back and read them now. They were provided to give you a more detailed grounding without disturbing the flow of each chapter.

- Feel good about yourself! You have nearly finished reading what for many would be an alarming, challenging set of ideas.

Chapter 17
Bibliography, References, Web sites and Organisations

Literature is the one place in any society where, within the secrecy of our own heads, we can hear voices talking about everything in every possible way. (Salman Rushdie)

The list is divided into chapters, but inevitably some resources are relevant to more than one chapter. This listing was correct at the time of its compilation, but inevitably will become out of date in time. This especially applies to URLs. I maintain up-to-date links with many of the sites mentioned from within my own Web pages, the address of which can be found in the Introduction list.

Most Pagan organisations request that you send a stamped addressed envelope or two International Reply Coupons when you write, if you require a reply. Most of the organisations listed are run by volunteers in their own time, so please allow them some time to reply.

I have no connection with the majority of resources listed, and they do not therefore necessarily represent my views. Although they are presented in good faith I can take no responsibility for the results of you using them. I have always been captivated by the idea of the Unseen University magical library in Terry Pratchett's (supposedly fictional) *Discworld* novels. Many of the books have to be chained down to stop them flying and exploding on contact with others, and the librarian was turned to an orang-utan when things got out of control. I would like to think that this collection was capable of producing the same effect.

Introduction
References
Moorey, Teresa, *Paganism – a beginner's guide* (Hodder and Stoughton, 1996)
Jones, Prudence, and Pennick, Nigel, *A History of Pagan Europe* (Routledge, 1995)
'What is Paganism?' leaflet, (The Pagan Federation, 2000)

Other Recommended Books
Anon, *Paganism Information Pack* (The Pagan Federation, 1996)
Crowley, Vivianne, *The Principles of Paganism* (Thorsons, 1995)
Harvey, Graham, and Hardman, Charlotte, *Paganism Today* (republished as *Pagan Pathways* in 2000) (Thorsons, 1996)
Herbert, Kathleen, *Looking for the Lost Gods of England* (Anglo Saxon, 1994)
Hutton, Ronald, *Pagan Religions of the Ancient British Isles: their nature and legacy* (Blackwells, 1991)
Ross, Ann, *Pagan Celtic Britain* (Constable, 1992)

Recommended Web sites
Covenant of the Goddess www.cog.org
Critical analysis of Wiccan claims www.geocities.com/wicca_hoax
Pagan Alliance (Australia) www.geocities.com/Athens/Thebes/4320/
Pagan Religion www.paganreligion.co.uk
The Pagan Federation www.paganfed.org
Pete Jennings Homepages www.gippeswic.demon.co.uk
UK Pagan Links www.ukpaganlinks.co.uk

Recommended Organisations
Circle, PO Box 219, Mount Horab, WI 535572, USA
Covenant of the Goddess, PO Box 1226, Berkeley, CA 94701, USA
Pagan Alliance of Australia, PO Box 406, Carlton South, VIC 3053, Australia
The Fellowship of Isis, Clonegal Castle, Enniscorthy, Eire
The Green Circle, PO Box 280, Maidstone, Kent ME16 0UL England
The Pagan Federation, BM Box 7097, London, WC1N 3XX England

Chapter 1 – Festivals and Rites of Passage
References
Kemp, Anthony, *Witchcraft and Paganism Today* (Michael O'Mara, 1993)

Sermon, Richard, *English Dance and Song magazine* (EFDSS, Vol. 53, No. 1, Spring 2001)
Starhawk, *The Spiral Dance* (HarperCollins, 1979)

Other Recommended Books
Howard, Michael, *The Sacred Ring: The Pagan origins of British folk festivals and customs* (Capall Bann, 1995)
Moorey, Teresa, and Brideson, Jane, *Wheel of the Year* (Hodder and Stoughton, 1997)

Recommended Websites
Tybol Astrological Almanac
     http://ourworld.compuserve.com/homepages/Tybol

Chapter 2 – Sacred Sites

References
Anderson, William, and Hicks, Clive, *Green Man: The Archetype of our Oneness with the Earth* (HarperCollins, 1990)
Bord, Janet and Colin, *The Secret Country* (Elek, 1976)
Farrar, Janet and Stewart, *The Witches' Goddess* (Robert Hale, 1996)
Harvey, Graham, and Hardman, Charlotte, *Paganism Today* (Thorsons, 1996: republished as *Pagan Pathways* in 2000)
Heselton, Phillip, *Secret Places of the Goddess* (Capall Bann, 1995)
Lethbridge, TC, *Gogmagog: The Buried Gods* (Routledge, 1957)
Pennick, Nigel, *Mazes and Labyrinths* (Robert Hale, 1990)
Stewart, RJ, *Power Within the Land* (Element, 1992)
Watkins, Alfred, *The Old Straight Track* (Abacus, 1974)

Other Recommended Books
Michell, John, *The View over Atlantis* (Thames and Hudson, 2001)

Recommended Websites
Third Stone www.thirdstone.demon.co.uk/home.htm
Council of British Archaeology www.britarch.ac.uk
Greenleaf/Robin's Greenwood Gang www.greenleaf.demon.co.uk
Rollrights Trust www.rollright.demon.co.uk

Recommended Organisations
I am deeply indebted to Andy Norfolk of ASLaN for his invaluable advice within this chapter, and permission to quote from an unpublished article.
ASLaN – Ancient Sacred Landscape Network, The Cottage, Crowan, Praze, Camborne, Cornwall TR14 9NB
Companions of the Chalice Well Trust, Chilkwell St, Glastonbury, Somerset BA6 8DD
Dragon Network, 23b Pepys Rd, New Cross, London SE14 5SA
Greenwood Guardians, 35 Carnavon Rd, Leyton, London E10 6DW
Olgar Trust, BM Olgar, London WC1N 3XX

Chapter 3 – Hereditary and Traditional Witchcraft

References

Bourne, Lois, *Dancing with Witches* (Robert Hale, 1988)

Dekker, Ford, and Rowley, ed. Kinney, F, *The Witch of Edmonton (a play of 1658)* (New Mermaid, 1998)

Fraser, James G, *The Golden Bough* in 13 volumes (Macmillan Press, 1936)

Gardner, Gerald B, *Witchcraft Today* (Rider, 1954: republished by Magickal Childe, 1980)

Green Egg Magazine, Vol. viii, no. 69 of 1975

Murray, Margaret, *The Witch Cult in Western Europe* (Oxford University Press, 1962)

Hutton, Ronald, *The Triumph of the Moon* (Oxford University Press, 2000)

Jones, Prudence, and Matthews, Caitlin, *Voices from the Circle* (Aquarius, 1990)

Leland, Charles G, *Aradia* (David Nutt, 1899, republished by Deosil Dance, 1991)

Liddell, WE, and Howard, Michael, *The Pickingill Papers* (Capall Bann, 1994)

Pennick, Nigel, *The Secrets of East Anglian Magic* (Hale, 1995)

Ryall, Rhiannon, *West Country Wicca* (Capall Bann, 1999)

Steele, Tony, *Rites and Rituals of Traditional Witchcraft* (Capall Bann, 2001)

Steele, Tony, *Water Witches* (Capall Bann, 1998)

Summers, Montague, *The History of Witchcraft* (Mystic Press, 1925)

Other Recommended Books

Adler, Margot, *Drawing Down the Moon* (Beacon, 1986)

Crowley, Vivianne, *The Principles of Wicca* (Thorsons, 1997)

Crowley, Vivianne, *Wicca: Old Religion in a new millennium* (Thorsons, 1996)

Guilley, Rosemary E, *The Encyclopedia of Witches and Witchcraft* (Checkmark, 1999)

Harrison, Michael, *The Roots of Witchcraft* (Tandem, 1975)

Hutton, Ronald, *The Stations of the Sun* (Oxford University Press, 1996)

Leek, Sybil, *The Complete Art of Witchcraft* (Leslie Frewin, 1975)

Leek, Sybil, *The Diary of a Witch* (Leslie Frewin, 1975)

Moorey, Teresa, *Witchcraft: a beginner's guide* (Hodder Headway, 1996)

Morgan, Keith, *Traditional Wicca* (Deosil Dance, 1990)

Various, *Witchcraft Information Pack* (The Pagan Federation, 1996)

West, Kate, *The Real Witches' Handbook* (HarperCollins, 2001)

Recommended Web sites

Best Witches (Witch Trials) www.rci.rutgers.edu/~jup/witches

Children of Artemis (Networking) www.witchcraft.org

New England Covens of Traditionalist Witches www.NECTW.org

Ordo Anno Mundi and Oera Linda Book www.oam.clara.net

Twisted Tree http://ourworld.compuserve.com/homepages/twisted_tree

Wiccan Rede http://wildideas.net/temple/library/redepoem.html
Witches Voice (Witchvox) www.witchvox.com

Recommended Organisations
Children of Artemis, BM Artemis, London, WC1N 3XX
North Star, BM Northstar, London WC1N 3XX
The Museum of Witchcraft, The Harbour, Boscastle, Cornwall PL35 0AE
Wicca Study Group, BM Deosil, London, WC1N 3XX

Chapter 4 – Gardnerian Witchcraft

References
Farrar, Janet and Stewart, *The Witches' Way* (Robert Hale, 1990)
Gardner, Gerald B, *High Magic's Aid* (Michael Houghton, 1949; repub-
    lished as Pentacle Enterprises, 1999)
Heselton, Phillip, *Wiccan Roots: Gerald Gardner and the modern witch-
    craft revival* (Capall Bann, 2000)
Hutton, Ronald, *The Triumph of the Moon* (Oxford University Press, 2000)

Other Recommended Books
Farrar, Janet and Stewart, *A Witch's Bible* (Robert Hale, 1997)
Gardner, Gerald B, *A Goddess Arrives* (I-H-O, 2000)
Gardner, Gerald B, *The Meaning of Witchcraft* (Aquarian Press, 1959)
Gardner, Gerald B, *Witchcraft Today* (Magickal Childe, 1980)
Valiente, Doreen, *An ABC of Witchcraft Past and Present* (Robert Hale, 1994)
Valente, Doreen, *Natural Magic* (Robert Hale, 1983)
Valiente, Doreen, *Witchcraft for Tomorrow* (Robert Hale, 1993)

Recommended Web sites
The first site has a chronological index of the Gardnerian family of traditions around the world.
www.gardnerian.net/beaufort/index.html
This includes Valiente's poetry and details of magical artefacts on exhibition.
www.doreenvaliente.com
Some personal history of Gardner.
www.themystica.com/mystica/articles/g/gardner_gerald_b.html
Photos of Gardner, Alex and Maxine Sanders and Gavin Bone.
http://gofree.indigo.ie/~wicca/person.htm
General Gardneriana www.avalonia.co.uk

Chapter 5 – Alexandrian Wicca

References
Farrar, Janet and Stewart, *Eight Sabbats for Witches* (Robert Hale, 1981)
Farrar, Janet and Stewart, *The Life and Times of a Modern Witch* (Piatkus,
    1987)
Farrar, Stewart, *What Witches Do* (P. Davies, 1971; 2nd edn., Phoenix, 1983;
    3rd edn; Robert Hale, 1991)

Harvey, Graham, and Hardman, Charlotte, *Paganism Today* (Thorsons, 1995: republished as *Pagan Pathways* in 2001)

Other Recommended Books
Crowther, Patricia, *Lid off the Cauldron* (Capall Bann, 1998)
Johns, June, *King of the Witches* (Peter Davies, 1969)

Recommended Web sites
Galdraheim Coven www.shamana.co.uk/galdraheim
Hexagon Archives www.hexagonarchive.com
Janus Gate http://reubes.aol.com/janus59/index.htm

Chapter 6 – Later Offshoots, Including Seax and Progressive Witchcraft

References
Buckland, Raymond, *The Tree*: *the Complete Book of Saxon Witchcraft* (Samuel Weiser, 1974)
Rainbird, Karin and Rankine, David, *Magick Without Peers* (Capall Bann, 1995)
Rainbird, Karin, *Talking Stick Magical Directory* (Talking Stick Publications, 1993)

Other Recommended Books
Buckland, Raymond, *Buckland's Complete Book of Witchcraft* (Llewellyn, 1986)

Recommended Web sites
Witches Voice (Witchvox) www.witchvox.com

Chapter 7 – Hedgewitch Traditions

References
Beth, Rae, *Hedgewitch* (Robert Hale, 1992)
Green, Marion, *The Elements of Natural Magic* (Element Books, 1997)
Green, Marion, *A Witch Alone: 13 Moons to master natural magic* (Thorsons, 1991)

Recommended Organisations
Invisible College, Marion Green, PO Box 42, Bath BA1 1ZN

Chapter 8 – Druidry

References
Harvey, Graham, and Hardman, Charlotte, *Paganism Today* (Thorsons, 1995: republished as *Pagan Pathways* in 2001)
Jones, Prudence, and Matthews, Caitlin, *Voices from the Circle* (Aquarius, 1990)
Smith, David, *Druidry Information Pack* (Pagan Federation, 2000)
Worthington, Cairistonia, *A beginner's guide to Druids* (Hodder and Stoughton, 1999)

Other Recommended Books
Aburrow, Yvonne, *The Enchanted Forest: The Magical Lore of Trees* (Capall Bann, 1993)
Chadwick, Nora, *The Celts* (Penguin, 1997)
Gomm, Phillip Carr, *The Druid Renaissance* (Thorsons, 1996)
Green, Miranda J, *Exploring the Worlds of the Druids* (Thames and Hudson, 1997)
Matthews, Caitlin, *Elements of the Celtic Tradition* (Element Books, 1996)
Matthews, Caitlin, *Elements of the Druid Tradition* (Element Books, 1996)
Matthews, John, *The Druid Source Book* (Ward Lock, 1997)
Nichols, Ross, *The Book of Druidry* (Thorsons, 1992)
Orr, Emma Restall, *Principles of Druidry* (Thorsons, 1998)
Orr, Emma Restall, *Spirits of the Sacred Grove* (Thorsons, 1998)
Pennick, Nigel, *Ogham and Coelbren: Mystic signs and symbols of the Celtic Druids* (Capall Bann, 2000)
Rees and Brindley, *Celtic Heritage* (Thames and Hudson, 1973)

Recommended Websites
Ar nDraiocht Fein www.adf.org
Bonewits Listing of Druid contacts www.neopagan.net/CurrentDruidGroups.HTML
OBOD www.druidry.org

Recommended Organisations
Ancient Order of Druids, 23 Thornsett Rd, London SE20 YXB
Ar nDraiocht Fein, PO Box 516, E Syracuse, NY 13057, USA
The British Druid Order, PO Box 29, St Leonards on Sea, East Sussex TN 37 7YP
Druid Clan of Dana, 7b Northover, Glastonbury, Somerset, BA6 8AA
Druid College of Albion, BM Stargrove, London WC1N 3XX
Druids of Albion, PO Box 8513, Ardrossan, Ayrshire KA22 8YE
Glastonbury Order of Druids, Dove House, Barton St. David, Somerset
Insular Order of Druids, Labyrinth, 2 Victoria Rd South, Southsea, Hants PO5 2DF
Loyal Arthurian Warband, AWEN, BM GAIA, London WC1N 3XX
Order of Bards, Ovates and Druids, PO Box 1333, Lewes, East Sussex BM7 7ZG

Chapter 9 – Asatru and the Northern Tradition
References
Aswynn, Freya, *Northern Mysteries and Magic* (Llewellyn, 2000 previously published as *The Leaves of Yggdrassil*)
Blain, Jenny, *Wights and Ancestors* (Wyrds Well, 2000)
Fitch, Ed, *The Rites of Odin* (Llewellyn, 1990)

Flowers, Stephen, *The Galdrabók, an Icelandic Grimoire* (Samuel Weiser, 1989)

Gundarsson, Kvendulf, *Teutonic Magic* (Llewellyn, 1990)

Gundarsson, Kvendulf, *Teutonic Religion* (Llewellyn, 1993)

Jennings, Pete, *The Norse Tradition: a beginner's guide* (Hodder Headway, 1998)

Jennings, Pete, *Northern Tradition Information Pack* (Pagan Federation, 2000)

Pennick, Nigel, *Practical Magic in the Northern Tradition* (Thoth, 1994)

Thorsson, Edred, *A Book of Troth* (Llewellyn, 1992)

Thorsson, Edred, *At the Well of the Wyrd* (Samuel Weiser, 1988)

Thorsson, Edred, *Futhark, a handbook of Rune Magic* (Samuel Weiser, 1984)

Thorsson, Edred, *Runelore* (Samuel Weiser, 1987)

Other Recommended Books

Aswynn, Freya, *Principles of the Runes* (Thorsons, 2000)

Crossley-Holland, Kevin, *Norse Myths* (Hodder Wayland, 1995)

Davidson, HR Ellis, *Gods and Myths of Northern Europe* (Penguin, 1990)

Davidson, Hilda Ellis, *Roles of the Northern Goddess* (Routledge, 1998)

Fries, Jan, *Helrunar: a manual of rune magick* (Mandrake, 1997)

Griffiths, Bill, *Aspects of Anglo-Saxon Magic* (Anglo Saxon, 1996)

Howard, Michael, *The Mysteries of the Runes* (Capall Bann, 1994)

King, Bernard. *The Elements of the Runes* (Element Books, 1993)

Larrington, Carolyne, *Poetic Edda* (Oxford University Press, 1999)

Linsell, Tony, *Anglo Saxon Runes* (Anglo Saxon, 1992)

Page, RI, *Reading the past: Runes* (British Museum, 1987)

Pennick, Nigel, *The Complete Illustrated Guide to Runes* (Element Books, 1999)

Peterson, Dr James, *The Enchanted Alphabet* (Aquarian Press, 1988)

Rodrigues, Louis R, *Anglo Saxon Verse Charms, Maxims and Heroic Legends* (Anglo Saxon, 1993)

Simek, Rudolf, *Dictionary of Northern Mythology* (D.S. Brewer, 1996)

Stone, Alby, *Ymirs flesh* (Heart of Albion, 1997)

Various, *The Sagas of the Icelanders* (Penguin, 1997)

Young, Jean, *Prose Edda of Snorri Sturlson* (University of California, 1964)

Recommended Web sites

Anglo Saxon Books www.asbooks.co.uk

Asatru Offerings http://odhinndis.freeyellow.com

Barbarian www.wizardrealm.com/norse/index.html

Freya Aswynn www.aswynn.co.uk

Heathen Europe www.geocities.com/heatheneurope

Hrafnar www.hrafnar.org

Irminsul Aettir www.irminsul.org

Jorvik Viking Centre www.jorvik-viking-centre.co.uk

Midgards Web www.astradyne.co.uk/midgard
Norse Myths www.ugcs.caltech.edu/~cherryne/mythology
Ring of Troth www.thetroth.org
Valkyries www.geocities.com/Heartland/Ranch/6604/Valkyrie.html
Viking Heritage http://viking.hgo.se
Wodanesdag www.bcsupernet.com/users/wodan/index.htm

Recommended Organisations
Asatru Alliance, PO Box 961, Payson, AZ 85547 USA
Asatru Folk Assembly, PO Box 445, Nevada City, CA 95959, USA
Hammarens Ordens Sallskap, 37 Somerset Rd, Irby, Wirral, England CH1 8SN
Jorvik Viking Centre, Coppergate, York YO1 9WT (Tel. 01904 643211)
Odinshof, BM Tercel, London, WC1N 3XX
Ring of Troth, BM Troth, London WC1N 3XX
Ring of Troth, PO Box 18812, Austin, Texas 78760, USA
The English Companions, Box 4336, London, WC1N 3XX

Chapter 10 – Shamanism

References
Artos, *Pagan Dawn* magazine, Issue No. 138, Spring 2001
Bates, Brian, *The Way of Wyrd* (Arrow, 1983)
Bates, Brian, *The Wisdom of Wyrd* (Rider, 1996)
Castaneda, Carlos, *A Journey to Ixtlan* (Simon and Schuster, 1972)
Clifton, Chas S, *Witchcraft and Shamanism* (Llewellyn, 1994)
Halifax, Joan, *Shamanic Voices* (Dutton, 1979)
Harner, Michael, *The Way of the Shaman* (Harper and Row, 1980)
Hultkrantz, Ake, *Shamanic Healing and Ritual Drama* (Crossroad, 1997)
Jennings, Pete, and Sawyer, Pete, *Pathworking* (Capall Bann, 1993)
Jones, Prudence, and Matthews, Caitlin, *Voices from the Circle* (Aquarius, 1990)
MacLellan, Gordon, *Sacred Animals* (Capall Bann, 1997)
MacLellan, Gordon, *Shamanism* (Piatkus, 1999)
Rutherford, Leo, *Principles of Shamanism* (Thorsons, 1996)

Other Recommended Books
Castaneda, Carlos, *A Separate Reality* (Simon and Schuster, 1971)
Castaneda, Carlos, *Tales of Power* (Simon and Schuster, 1974)
Castaneda, Carlos, *The Teachings of Don Juan* (University of California, 1968)
Drury, Neville, *Elements of Shamanism* (Element Books, 1996)
Matthews, Caitlin, *Singing the Soul Back Home* (Element Books, 1995)
Matthews, John, *The Celtic Shaman* (Element Books, 1991)
Meadows, Kenneth, *The Medicine Way* (Element Books, 1990)
Moorey, Teresa, *Shamanism: a beginner's guide* (Hodder Headway, 1997)

Recommended Web sites

Carlos Castaneda www.castaneda.com

Collection of shamanism essays from around the world www.boudicca.de

Core Shamanism, including Spirit Talk magazine + Scandinavian Centre for Shamanic Studies + London Open Drumming www.users.dircon.co.uk/ ~snail

Dance of the Deer Foundation (USA) www.shamanism.com

Deoxy (Peru/Ecuador) www.deoxy.org/shamanism.htm

Eagles Wing (UK) www.shamanism.co.uk

Earthsongs (Canada) www.faeryshaman.org/earthsong.htm

Flight of the Condor – contemporary shamanism www.kondor.de

Forbidden Fruit (USA/South America/Nepal) www.theforbiddenfruit. com

Foundation for Shamanic Studies (Michael Harner) www.shamanism.org

Huna Shamanism (Hawaii) www.huna.net

Metista (USA) www.metista.com

Russian Culture (Russian/Siberian) http://russianculture.about.com

Raven Lodge (UK) www.shamana.co.uk

Sacred Hoop www.sacredhoop.org

Sacred Trust (UK courses) www.sacredtrust.org

Shaman Institute (USA) www.shamaninstitute.com

Shamanka (UK) www.shamanka.org

Spirit Quest Amazonian Journeys www.biopark.org

Three Worlds (Ireland) http://indigo.ie/~imago/3worlds

Twin Shaman (USA) www.newgaia.com

Recommended Organisations

Eagles Wing, 58, Westbere Road, London NW2 3RU (Tel. (44) 0207 435 8174)

Society of Celtic Shamans, PO Box 233, Harrison Hot Springs, BC, Canada VOM 1KO

Chapter 11 – Male and Female Mystery Groups and Psychic Questers

References

Adler, Margot, *Drawing Down the Moon* (Beacon, 1986)

Baigent, Michael, Leigh, Richard, and Lincoln, Henry, *The Holy Blood and the Holy Grail* (Arrow, 1996)

Bly, Robert, *Iron John: a book about men* (Element, 1999)

Budapest, Z, *Holy Book of Women's Mysteries* (Harper and Row, 1990)

Collins, Andrew, *The Black Alchemist* (ABC Books, 1988)

Crowley, Vivianne, *The Phoenix from the Flame: Paganism in the New Age* (Thorsons, 1995)

Estes, Clarissa Pinkola, *Women who run with wolves: contacting the Power of the Wild Woman* (Rider, 1998)

Graves, Robert, *The White Goddess* (Faber & Faber, 1948)

Harvey, Graham, and Hardman, Charlotte, *Paganism Today* (Thorsons, 1996: republished as *Pagan Pathways* in 2000)

Hutton, Ronald, *Pagan Religions of the Ancient British Isles: their nature and legacy* (Blackwells, 1991)

Sjoo, M, and Mor, B, *The Great Cosmic Mother* (HarperCollins, 1991)

Starhawk, *The Spiral Dance* (HarperCollins, 1979)

Stewart, RJ, *Celebrating the Male Mysteries* (Arcadia, 1991)

Stewart, RJ, *The Way of Merlin* (Aquarian Press, 1991)

Other Recommended Books

Bly, R, and Rowan, J, *Choirs of God: Revisioning Masculinity* (Mandala, 1991)

Farrar, Janet and Stewart, *The Witches' God* (Robert Hale, 1995)

Farrar, Janet and Stewart, *The Witches' Goddess* (Robert Hale, 1996)

Fitch, Eric, *In Search of Herne the Hunter* (Capall Bann, 1994)

George, Demetra, *Mysteries of the Dark Moon: the healing power of the dark Goddess* (HarperSanFrancisco, 1992)

Gray, Miranda, *Red Moon: Understanding and using the gifts of the menstrual cycle* (Element Books, 1994)

Jackson, Nigel, *The Call of the Horned Piper* (Capall Bann, 1996)

Jackson, Nigel, *Masks of Misrule: the Horned God and his cult in Europe* (Capall Bann, 1996)

Matthews, Caitlin, *Voices of the Goddess: a chorus of sybils* (Aquarian Press, 1991)

Moorey, Teresa and Howard, *Pagan Gods for Today's Man: a beginner's guide* (Headway, 1997)

O'Regan, Vivian, *Pillar of Isis: a practical manual on the mysteries of the Goddess* (Aquarian Press, 1993)

Raphael, Melissa, *Introducing Theology: Discourse on the Goddess* (Pilgrim, 2000)

Richardson, Alan, *Earth God Rising: the return of the male mysteries* (Llewellyn, 1991)

Rowan, John, *Horned God: Feminism and men as wounding and healing* (Routledge, 1987)

Sinclair-Wood, Lyn, *Creating Form from the Mist: wisdom of women in Celtic myth and culture* (Capall Bann, 1999)

Walker, Barbara, *The Women's Encyclopaedia of Myths and Secrets* (Pandora, 1996)

Chapter 12 – Eclectic Paganism and Foreign Traditions

Recommended Books

Ames, Delano, *Egyptian Mythology* (Paul Hamlyn, 1965)

Budge, EA Wallis, *The Egyptian Book of the Dead* (Dover, 1967)

Green, Miranda J, *The Gods of Roman Britain* (Shire, 1983)

Jacq, Christian, *Magic and Mystery in Ancient Egypt* (Souvenir Press, 1998)
Pinch, Geraldine, *Magic in Ancient Egypt* (British Museum Press, 1994)
Rigaud, Milo, *Secrets of Voodoo* (City Lights, 1985)
Starhawk, *The Spiral Dance* (HarperCollins, 1979)
Wyley, Graham, *The Illustrated Guide to Witchcraft* (Parkgate,1998)

Recommended Web sites
Vodoun Culture www.geocities.com/Athens/Delphi/5319/
Voodoo Encyclopedia www.arcana.com/voodoo
Vodou Page http://members.aol.com/racine125/
Voodoo Server www.nando.net/prof/caribe/voodoo.html

Recommended Organisations
Egyptian Mystery Tradition, Temple of Khem, c/o Ignotus Press (Dept. ToK), BM Writer, London WC1N 3XX

Chapter 13 – Magical Theory and its Ethics

References
Crowley, Aleister, *The Magical Record of the Beast 666 and Liber Legis, Book of the Law* (Samuel Weiser, 1976)
Farrar, Janet and Stewart, *The Witches' Way* (Hale, 1990)
Hutton, Ronald, *The Triumph of the Moon* (Oxford University Press, 2000)
Levi, Eliphas, *The History of Magic* (trans. A. E. Waite: Rider, 1913)
MacLellan, Gordon, *Sacred Animals* (Capall Bann, 1997)
Valiente, Doreen, *Witchcraft for Tomorrow* (Robert Hale, 1993)

Other Recommended Books
Booth, Martin, *A Magick Life: a biography of Aleister Crowley* (Hodder and Stoughton, 2000)
Crowley, Aleister, *Magick in Theory and Practice* (Dover, 1986)
Freke and Gandy, *The Hermetica* (Piatkus, 1998)
Fries, Jan, *Visual Magic* (Mandrake, 1991)
Grant, Kenneth, *The Magical Revival* (Frederick Muller.,1972)
Hawkins, Jaq B, *Understanding Chaos Magic* (Capall Bann, 1996)
Walker, Charles, *The Encyclopedia of Secret Knowledge* (Rider, 1995)

Recommended Web sites
Chaos Matrix www.chaosmatrix.com
John Dee Society www.johndee.org
OTO Links http://web2/airmail.net/otontex/links.html
Pictures of Spare www.banger.com/banger/spare/graf/index.html

Chapter 14 – Using Magic

References
Barrett, Francis, *The Magus* (Lackington, Allen, 1801; republished by Citadel, 1975)
Bonewits, Isaac, *Real Magic* (Samuel Weiser, 1989)

Carroll, Peter J, *Liber Null and Psychonaut* (Samuel Weiser, 1987)

Farrar, Janet and Stewart, *The Witches' Way* (Robert Hale, 1990)

Fortune, Dion, *The Sea Priestess* (Wyndham, 1976)

Grant, Kenneth, *Images and Oracles of Austin Spare* (Frederick Muller, 1975)

Hine, Phil, *Chaos Condensed* (Phoenix, 1992)

Levi, Eliphas, *The History of Magic* (trans. A. E. Waite: Rider, 1913)

Sherwin, Ray, *The Book of Results* (Revelations 23 Press, 1992)

Spare, Austin Osman, *Anathema of Zos* (Black Moon, 1985)

Wilson, Steve, *Chaos Ritual* (Neptune Press, 1994)

Other Recommended Books

Ashcroft-Nowicki, Dolores, *The Ritual Magic Workbook* (Aquarian Press, 1986)

Brodie, Jan, *Psychic Self Defence* (Capall Bann, 1995)

Fortune, Dion, *Moon Magic* (Wyndham, 1976)

Levi, Eliphas, *Transcendental Magic* (Senate, 1995)

Mathers, M, and Liddell, S, *The Goetia: the lesser key of Solomon the King* (Samuel Weiser, 1995)

Pennick, Nigel, *Way of Natural Magic* (Thorsons, 2001)

Regardie, Israel, *The Foundations of Practical Magic* (Aquarian Press, 1982)

Regardie, Israel, *The Golden Dawn* (Llewellyn, 1989)

Regardie, Israel and others, *A Garden of Pomegranates* (Llewellyn, 1999)

Spare, Austin Osman, *Book of Satyrs* (Venus, 1989)

Spare, Austin Osman, *The Focus of Life* (Morland, 1921)

Recommended Web sites

Some key chaos texts http://user.sezampro.yu/~babbage/chaolib.html

Thelemic/Reichian/Chaos/Ceremonial/Chaos/Golden Dawn/Qabala/OTO/Tantra texts www.lysator.liu.se/occult/index.html

Chapter 15 – Where Do We Go From Here?

References

Arnold, Matthew, *Essays in Criticism* second series, 'The Study of Poetry' (1888)

Bell, Clive, *Art* (1914) quoted in *Oxford Dictionary of Literary Quotations* (Oxford University Press, 1999)

O'Casey, Sean, *The Plough and the Stars* (1926), quoted in *Oxford Dictionary of Literary Quotations* (Oxford University Press, 1999)

Orphic Hymn, translation by Apostolos N Athanassakis, quoted in Olsen, Carl, *Book of the Goddess Past and Present* (Crossroad, 1992)

Stevens, Wallace, *Adagia* (1957)

Other Recommended Books

Zell, Oberon, and Davis, Pete, *The Other People* (Pathfinder Press, 1994)

Recommended Web sites

LifeRites Organisation (arranges rites of passage) www.liferites.org
My own web site with links to many other Pagan pages
    www. gippeswic.demon.co.uk
The Pagan Library set of responses for Evangelists
    www.paganlibrary.com/ fundies
Two major suppliers of new and second-hand occult books:
Atlantis Bookshop www.atlantisbookshop.demon.co.uk
Caduceus Books www.caduceus.demon.co.uk

Recommended Organisations

LifeRites, Gwndwn Mawr, Trelech, Carmarthenshire SA33 6SA

Chapter 16 – The Future of Paganism

References

Adler, Margot, *Drawing Down the Moon* (Beacon, 1986)
Bates, Brian, *The Way of Wyrd* (Arrow, 1983)
Capey, Cynthia, *Faiths in Focus* (Suffolk College, 1993)
Capey, Cynthia, *Finding our Way and Sharing our Stories* (Suffolk College, 1995)
Crowley, Vivianne, *The Phoenix from the Flame: Paganism in the New Age* (Thorsons, 1995)
La Fontaine, Prof. JS, *The Extent and Nature of Organised and Ritual Abuse* (HMSO, 1994)
Starhawk, *The Spiral Dance* (HarperCollins, 1979)

Other Recommended Books

Dahl, Roald, *The Witches* (Puffin, 1985)
Pratchett, Terry, the *Discworld* series of books (Corgi, 1985 onwards)
Rowling, JK, the *Harry Potter* series of books (Bloomsbury, 1997 onwards)
Sulak, J and Vale, V, *Modern Pagans* (RE/Search Publications, 2001)
Tolkien, JRR, *The Lord of the Rings* (HarperCollins, 1995)

Recommended Websites

Interfaith in the USA – source of quote by Hans Kung www.interfaith.org

Magazines

There are a large number of magazines circulating, from occasional, locally-focused short-lived two-page newsletters to glossy, long-established international quarterly editions. It is not practicable to give details on every one here, but I list below a selection of those of national level direct interest, which have been in existence for some time. Inevitably, even the most professional ones are produced as 'labours of love' by volunteers, so please send a stamped addressed envelope or IRC when enquiring, and be prepared for a less than instantaneous response.

The Cauldron (Wicca), M Howard, Caemorgan Cottage, Caemorgan Rd, Cardigan, Ceredigion, West Wales SA43 1QU *

Chaos International, BM Sorcery, London WC1N 3XX

Circle (General), PO Box 219, Mount Horeb, WI 53572 USA

Green Circular (Green Circle), PO Box 280, Maidstone ME16 OUL

Hidden Path (Gardnerian Wicca), PO Box 934, Kenosha WI 53141-0934 USA

Kabbalist (Cabbala), 25, Circle Gardens, Merton Park, London SW19 3JX

Kindred Spirit (General), Foxhole, Dartington, Totnes, Devon TQ9 6EB

Little Red Book (Directory of Pagan Resources and articles), PO Box 513, Preston, PR5 6UZ

Pagan Dawn (General – The Pagan Federation), BM Box 7097, London WC1N 3XX

Prediction (Astrology, New Age), Link House, Dingwall Ave, Croydon, Surrey CR9 2TA

Queer Spirit (Gay/Lesbian Pagans), Box QS, OUT! 4-7 Dorset St, Brighton BN2 1WA

Quest (Marion Green), BCM-SCL Quest, London, WC1N 3XX

Sacred Hoop (Shamanism), PO Box 16, Narberth, Pembrokeshire, Wales SA67 8YG

Sage Woman (Goddess), Blessed Bee Inc., PO Box 641, Point Arena, CA 95468-0099, USA

Shamans Drum, PO Box 97, Ashland OR 97520 USA

Witchcraft and Wicca, BM: Artemis, London WC1N 3XX

Wood and Water (Goddess), 77 Parliament Hill, London NW3 2TH

*Do not put magazine title or other Pagan indications on envelope, to protect the privacy of the correspondent.

Glossary

Abyss Primal void, which must be crossed (in the mind) within some Pagan paths. Also the starting point for Chaos Magic and theory.

Adept A person who is skilled at magic.

Adeptus Exemptus 9th Golden Dawn grade.

Adeptus Major 8th Golden Dawn grade.

Adeptus Minor 7th Golden Dawn grade.

Alchemist One who attempts physical change by combination of science and magic. In mediaeval times they popularly searched for the 'philosopher's stone', which would reputedly turn base metal to gold.

Alexandrian Witchcraft tradition started by Alex Sanders.

Altar Any platform made the focal point and working surface for ritual.

Amulet A non-specific good luck charm, usually worn on the person.

Animism A belief that every natural thing has a divine spark of life.

Asatru A faith in the Norse deities (see also **Northern Tradition**).

Astral planes A series of several levels of spiritual realms.

Athame A ritual knife, often black handled.

Awen All-pervading life current revered by the Druid traditions.

Bard A singer, storyteller, poet and musician. Also a key stage of Druidry.

Beltane Spring festival, May 1.

Berserker Norse warrior cult dedicated to the bear.

Blot Norse Tradition ritual.

Boline White-handled knife used for cutting herbs etc.

Book of Shadows A book of rituals and spells copied out by successive generations.

Brythonic Of the Welsh, Breton or Cornish speaking cultures.

Cabbala (also Qabbala) Hebrew magical system.

Cakes and Ale Pagan communal feast, which can comprise other food and drink.

Candomble Brazilian form of Voodoo.

Ceremonial Magicians Magicians who attempt magic by complex rituals, which they have to carry out to exact detail, involving a lot of magical tools.

Chakras Eastern belief in spiritual access points around the human body.

Chalice A ritual drinking vessel, which can be made of metal, horn or wood.

Chaos Magic A system that builds up from a void, rather than correspondences.

Cone of Power A group ritual's visualised form of collective magical power.

Co-Mason Masonic order with magical interests which admitted women members.

Correspondences Relationship between different colours, symbols, deities, plants, etc.

Coven A localised group of witches working together.

Craft Abbreviation for Craft of the Wise or Witchcraft.

Chthonic Of the Earth or Underworld.

Cunning Man Type of English male village magician.

Degree The level of accomplishment within a hierarchy of grades of witch.

Deity God, Goddess or a force beyond understanding of humans.

Deosil Sunwise or clockwise direction.

Dianic Female-only Pagan groups, who often worship the Goddess Diana.

Drawing Down the Moon Causing a priestess to become possessed by the Goddess.

Druid Celtic Pagan religious path, which includes Bards and Ovates.

Eclectic Drawing beliefs and practices from more than one tradition.

Elements In the Western traditions these are Air, Fire, Water, Earth and Spirit.

Enochian Magical language of Dr Dee, according to Mathers.

Evoking To encourage possession of one's body by a supernatural force.

Fetch A spirit sent from the body to do a task.

Fundamentalist Somebody who takes the basic texts of a religion as absolute truth.

Futhark A rune alphabet.

Fylga Norse term for a **fetch**.

Gaia Greek Goddess used to personify Mother Earth as a living entity.

Gardnerian Tradition of witchcraft started by Gerald Gardner.

Genius loci The spirit of the place.

Georgian Eclectic tradition of witchcraft started by George Patterson.

Gorsedd (plural Gorseddau) Public gathering of Bards within Druid tradition.

Gothi Male priest of the Northern Tradition.

Great Rite Magic accomplished by sexual intercourse.

Green Man A foliate figure with leaves exuding from the mouth or elsewhere.

Grimoire Collected book of spells and rituals, similar to Book of Shadows.

Gytha Priestess of the Northern Tradition.

Hamingja Norse guardian spirit.

Handfasting Pagan wedding rite.

Heathen Germanic term for a Pagan, or follower of rural-based older religions.

Hedgewitch A solo Witch belonging to no other particular tradition.

Hereditary A tradition of witchcraft transmitted through a family connection.

Hermetic Belief or magic based on Egyptian texts, used as a term by Crowley.

Hexancrafte Witchcraft tradition from the Netherlands.

High Magic Magic concerned with the development of the higher self and intellect.

Imbolc Celtic festival, around February 2.

Imitative Magic Attempting to create a magical act by imitating its action.

Initiation Starting a new spiritual path or higher level of an existing path.

Interfaith Members of one religion talking with members of other religions.

Intrafaith Members of various traditions of a general religion talking together.

Invoking To encourage a supernatural force to enter somebody else's body.

IOT Illuminatus Order of Thanateros.

Ipsissimus Twelfth and ultimate Golden Dawn grade.

Karma Eastern belief in the need to balance your actions.

Kiss, five-, seven- or ninefold A ritual act of kissing parts of the body of another witch.

Lares Roman name for household gods.

Left-Hand Path Generally destructive magic.

Ley Line Theory of energy currents and alignments of monuments within landscape.

Low Magic Practical everyday magic concerned with mundane matters.

Magic Causing change by projecting your will.

Magister 'Teacher' – male officer of certain types of witches' covens.

Magister Templi 10th Golden Dawn grade.

Magus 11th Golden Dawn grade, but also used for any higher-level magician.

Man in Black Same role as magister, a senior male officer for certain witches' covens.

Measure Length of twine measured around body of some witch initiates.

Mjollnir Thor's hammer, used in Northern Tradition rites to sanctify.

Monotheism Belief in a single God.

Moot A social meeting of Pagans, in pub or house, which may have a talk content.

Mystery Unknown, different from a secret in that it can only be experienced.

Neophyte Novice Golden Dawn grade.

Newbie New inexperienced Pagan.

Northern Tradition Anglo-Saxon and Norse Heathen path (also known as Asatru/Odinism).

Occult Religious secret or mystery.

Odinist Follower of Norse God Odin, but may also include others of same pantheon.

OGD Order of the Golden Dawn.

Ogham A Celtic way of writing onto the angled corner of wood or stone.

Ophidian Tradition based on Frisian *Oera Linda* book and led by Tony Steele.

Orlog Norse/Saxon theory of fate.

OTO *Ordo Templi Orientis.*

Ovate A stage of Druidry concerned with herb lore, healing and shamanistic practices.

Pagan Roman term for follower of old rural religions.

Pantheism Belief in an all-pervading natural life force.

Paradigm A set of beliefs and circumstances artificially created or invoked by Chaos Magicians for a single magical working.

Pathworking A creative visualisation meditation form.

Pentacle A platter marked with symbols to be used as a container within ritual.

Pentagram Five-pointed star symbol.

Philosophus 5th Golden Dawn grade.

Polarity Balancing out opposing forces, e.g. fire/water, black/white, sun/moon.

Polytheism Belief in many Gods and Goddesses.

Poppet A doll used to represent a person on which magic is to be worked.

Portal 6th Golden Dawn grade, and the lowest of the Inner Orders. Also entrance to magical space.

Power Animal Spirit guide and helper used by shamans.

Practicus 4th Golden Dawn grade.

Priapic After Priapus, a God with a large erect phallus.

Progressive Experimental tradition of witchcraft.

Proselytise To promote one's religious beliefs to others.

Psychopomp A figure or omen preceding a death.

Quarters Cardinal points of the compass.

Radical Faeries Gay American Pagan group.

Right Hand Path The use of magic for positive purposes.

Ritual Any repeated set of actions and/or words.

Runes Magical symbols and letters of the Asatru traditions.

Samhain Celtic New Year festival on October 31.

Santeria South American path mixing African Yoruba and Christian traditions.

Satanism A heretical reversal of the Christian religion. It is not part of Paganism.

Scourge A light whip, used within a few religious traditions.

Scribe Secretary/Treasurer of a **Seax** Wiccan coven.

Scrying Foreseeing the future by looking into a dark mirror or liquid.

Seax Saxon-based witchcraft tradition started by Buckland.

Shaman A person who travels within spirit realms to aid their community.

Sheila-na-Gig Female carving displaying genitals.

Sigil A written or painted magical symbol, usually with its meaning disguised.

Skyclad Naked.

Stang Forked stick representing the God.

Strega Italian Witch tradition.

Sweat Lodge A sauna/steam bath type of construction used in some spiritual practices, particularly Native American and some other shamanistic paths.

Sympathetic Magic See **Imitative Magic**.

Talisman An object magically prepared for a specific purpose.

Tantra Spiritual practices from the East, particularly those connected with yoga, body control and sacred sex.

Tarot A set of cards used for divination, ritual and meditation.

Thegn Leading officer in a **Seax** Wiccan coven.

Thelemic Relating to ancient Egyptian texts, but coined by Crowley for his beliefs.

Theoricus 3rd Golden Dawn grade.

Theosophy Knowledge of God, term used by Madame Blavatsky and her followers.

Traditional Pre-1950s witchcraft.

Transference Magic Magic performed by transferring sickness, spirit, etc., into an object which can be more easily manipulated, such as a stick or stone.

Triple Goddess The feminine divine in three phases: maiden, mother, crone.

Troth Asatru practice of being true to Gods and tribe and family.

Valknut Knot of the Slain, three interlocking triangles associated with Odin.

Vitki Shaman/runemaster of the Northern Tradition.

Volva Seeress of the Northern Tradition.

Voodoo/Vodoun Anglo-French Caribbean spiritual path drawing on African Obea practices and Christian saints.

Wand Any stick designated for projecting magic.

Wicca Originally post-1950s witchcraft, but sometimes now includes pre-1950s.

Wiccaning Ritual blessing and naming of a baby.

Widdershins Anti-clockwise or against the direction of the sun.

Witch A person who works magic through Pagan beliefs.

Witchcraft Term including all Witches, but not representing non-magical Pagans.

Woodwose Carved figure of wild man, generally with club and body markings.

Wyrd Idea of all lives and actions being pre-ordained and interconnected.

Yule Festival of midwinter, around December 21.

Zelator 2nd Golden Dawn grade.

Index